TERRY
DEARY'S
TERRIBLY TRUE
DISASTER STORIES

SCHOLASTIC

The facts behind these stories are true. However, they
have been dramatized to make them into gripping stories,
and some of the characters are fictitious.

Scholastic Children's Books,
Euston House, 24 Eversholt Street
London, NW1 1DB, UK

A division of Scholastic Ltd
London ~ New York ~ Toronto ~ Sydney ~ Auckland
Mexico City ~ New Delhi ~ Hong Kong

First published in the UK under the series title *True Stories* by
Scholastic Ltd, 1999

Typeset by Rapid Reprographics Ltd
Printed in the UK by CPI Bookmarque, Croydon, CR0 4TD

10 9 8 7 6 5 4 3

CONTENTS

INTRODUCTION

Every day, somewhere in the world, disasters happen. Sometimes they're great disasters that you may get to hear about in the news; usually they are so small, and so common, you will never know about them. And sometimes there are disasters that aren't disasters at all ... when a football team loses a game and the newspapers describe it as a "disaster". It isn't. No one was hurt, no one died.

There have been far more disasters than one book could ever record. But the most interesting ones are the ones that tell you something about the people involved. After all, you want to know how *you* would cope if you were faced with a dreadful threat.

Here's an example – test yourself.

There was a deadly plague in northern England in AD 693. The historian Bede was a monk at the time and the monks were all safe in their monastery; but the sick people of the town came to the monks for help. What would you do in that position? Be a hero/ine – open the doors and let in the plague? Or be a coward – bolt the doors and let the sufferers die in misery?

Well? What would you do?

And what did the monks do in that terrible time? Bede told of how they let the plague victims in and nursed them. As a result 80 of the monks died and only two survived. The dead were heroes.

Here are seven stories of both hero/ines who risked their lives and cowards who ran away. There are even stories of a villain who deliberately created a disaster and a couple of men whose stupidity allowed one to happen. How would you react? What sort of person are you? That's what you want to know.

The trouble is you will never *really* know until you actually face disaster yourself. The truth is that one person can be a hero/ine one day and a coward the next!

I've been in a gym when a boy climbed on the roof to get a ball; he stepped on a glass skylight and fell five metres to the ground, slashing his leg and chest open till the flesh was hanging off. While some of his friends ran off to be sick I was able to stay with him and hold him till the ambulance arrived. Looking back I guess that sounds quite a courageous thing to do. The boy survived.

But I'm not a hero. I know that because, many years later, I witnessed a car crash. A small red hatchback shot around a corner and headed towards me on the wrong side of the road. I stopped my car and watched in horror as it slid sideways, missed me and ploughed into the front porch of a house. I should have jumped out to see if I could help. I sat, clutching my steering-wheel in shock.

A man staggered out of the passenger door and ran up the road past my car. He was obviously a thief, running from his stolen car. I should have stopped him. I sat clutching my steering-wheel in shock. Then, from the wreckage I saw the driver slide over to the passenger's door, stagger out with blood streaming down his nose, and run off in the opposite direction. I sat clutching my steering-wheel in shock.

Hero one day, coward another.

So there are no easy answers. But the stories and the facts that surround them are fascinating.

THROUGH THE LIGHT

Sometimes disaster strikes and there is nothing anyone can do about it. No one can stop an earthquake or a flood, for example. But some disasters are caused by humans – by evil humans who set out to destroy others or by harmless men, women and children who simply got careless. What do you do to people who have caused the death of hundreds in a moment of stupidity?

The Quintinshill rail disaster, Scotland, May 1915

The judge wore a scarlet gown. It was the only splash of colour in the drab courtroom. The lawyers wore black and their wigs were dusty grey. The people in the public gallery wore funeral black. Some clutched black-edged handkerchiefs to their faces. The men in the dock wore black suits and white shirts with starched collars as colourless as their faces.

The judge cleared his throat and glared down at the accused man. "Perhaps, Mr Tinsley, we can hear your account of what happened on the day of the accident," he said, his voice paper dry.

The little man licked his lips and clutched at the worn wooden rail in front of him. Beside him the round-faced man with a

10

walrus moustache stared gloomily at the floor. He seemed afraid to look up and meet the stares of the people in the gallery. "I was at Gretna Station. Just about to go on duty at the Quintinshill signal-box when the telephone rang," he began. His voice was thin and trembling.

"Speak up," the judge snapped.

James Tinsley licked his lips again. "I was on the day shift and I was due to start at six a.m. The phone call was from Mr Meakin here," he said, and nodded at the silent man beside him. "He said the local passenger train would be stopping at the signal-box that morning. I could hop on it at Gretna and save myself the walk."

"So this local passenger train didn't usually stop at Quintinshill signal-box?" the judge asked, dipping a steel-nibbed pen in an ink bottle.

"No, sir. The express train to Glasgow usually went through first then the local train went through. But that morning ... the morning of the accident ... the Glasgow train was half an hour late. They decided to let the local train set off first. The Glasgow express would catch it up at Quintinshill signal-box. The local train would pull off on to one of the two side tracks to let the Glasgow Express through."

"And that's when you'd get off the local train?" the judge asked. He scratched a simple plan on to his notepaper and nodded.

"Yes, sir. We pulled in about half-past six."

The judge looked up sharply. "I thought you started work at six!"

"I was *supposed* to. But George here said he'd cover for me till I got there," the little man replied and nodded his head towards his silent partner.

"Is that allowed?"

James Tinsley's tongue flickered over his lips like a snake tasting the air. "No, sir."

The judge nodded. "You broke the rules."

"Yes, sir. We did it to help each other out. I would do the same for George here."

"And you were never caught?"

"No, sir. There's a record book. It's called the Train Register. I had to sign in at six and make a note in the register of all the trains that went past Quintinshill. So, George here would make a note of the trains, and I copied them into the register in my handwriting when I arrived."

The judge shook his head. "Sounds like a couple of schoolboys cheating at homework. But it's more serious than that, isn't it, Mr Tinsley?" The little signalman didn't answer. The judge went on. "So, on the morning of the accident your local train arrived at the signal-box and pulled on to one of the side tracks?"

"No, sir."

"No? Why not?"

"Because there was already a train on each siding. Goods trains," Tinsley explained.

"So where did the local train go to get out of the way of the express?" the judge asked, looking down at his sketch.

"It crossed over on to the other main line. The line that trains used to go south to London."

The judge frowned. "Can you do that? Isn't it dangerous?"

"We do it all the time, sir," Tinsley said eagerly. "It's not against the rules. It's safe ... usually."

"I see. So the local train was on the London line, the goods trains were on the sidings and the Glasgow line was clear for the express?"

"Yes, sir."

"So what went wrong?"

Tinsley cleared his throat. The crowds in the gallery seemed to lean forward to listen. "The fireman from the local train and the guards from the goods trains went to the signal-box with me while we waited for the Glasgow express to go through."

"The guards left their trains?" The judge asked. "Surely that is against the railway rules, isn't it?"

"Yes, sir. They can only leave in an emergency."

"And what was this emergency? Well, Mr Tinsley? I'm sure the ladies and gentlemen of the court would like to hear what it was that was so important that three men deserted their trains! Why did they go to the signal-box?"

Tinsley looked at George Meakin. Meakin didn't raise his eyes or make any move to help his friend. Tinsley clutched at the rail and muttered. The judge asked him to repeat it, louder. "They came up for a cup of tea."

The silence in the courtroom was complete. Finally the judge spoke. "I see. Three railwaymen, you and Mr Meakin, all in the signal-box. Three trains on the tracks below you. And you were drinking *tea*."

Tinsley nodded. "I was filling in the Train Register," he said quietly. "Mr Meakin was reading my morning paper."

"Very cosy," the judge said sourly. "Then the Glasgow express arrived, I suppose."

"No, sir. We got two messages. One said the Glasgow train was on its way – half an hour late. But that was all right. The Glasgow line was clear. It was … it was the second message that was the problem."

"And the second message said what?"

Tinsley spoke slowly. His voice was breaking but the silence was so heavy that everyone could hear him. "It said there was a London express on the way. A special army train full of troops."

"This troop train – this London express – was rushing towards you. It was speeding down the *London* line where your local train was standing! Couldn't you do anything to stop it?"

"Oh, yes, sir! We could have switched the signal to red."

"Red for danger?"

"Red for stop!"

"And why didn't you do that, Mr Tinsley? That's what this court wants to know," the judge said.

The signalman let go of the rail and spread his hands wide. "I don't know!"

There was a hiss of whispered talk from the gallery. The judge didn't bother to silence it, he simply raised his voice over the top of the horrified comments. "You gave a green signal to a London express when its line was blocked by the local train! You knew that, man! Surely you *knew* that!"

"I forgot!" the little signalman cried. "I forgot all about the local train."

The hiss of the spectators turned to a roar and the judge let it rise for a while. Words like "murderers" and "criminal" and "hang him" bounced off the dark oak panels round the courtroom. Finally the judge rapped on his bench. "Silence! I said silence! Silence or I will have this court cleared." At last the noise died and the red-robed judge was able to go on. "The London express smashed into the local train and killed hundreds of soldiers on board."

"No, sir," came a soft voice with a Scottish accent. George Meakin spoke for the first time. He looked up, wide eyes shadowed with dark pools like a man who hasn't slept for years.

He spoke like a man in a trance. "The London train hit the local train and pushed it back forty yards. The express tipped on its side and the carriages broke open – they were wooden carriages of course. Men tumbled out. Some were bleeding, some were crying, some at the back were unharmed. They were going into the wreckage to rescue their friends. It wouldn't have been so bad. It wouldn't! But ... but..."

The judge nodded. "There was the second express, wasn't there? The Glasgow express. The one that was half an hour late. You'd given a green light to that too, hadn't you?"

Meakin's round face was strained and grey. "We saw it all from the signal box! I called to James, I said, 'Stop the Glasgow train!' He switched the signal to red. But it was too late! It was already past the signal. We stood there in the box and we saw it all! First the London train ploughed into the local train and fell across the Glasgow track. Then the Glasgow express raced into the wreck of the London express! It was horrible! I'll have nightmares about it as long as I live!"

There was a roar of anger from the gallery. "At least you *will* live!" a woman screamed. "That's more than our men will! You murderer!"

Her cry was cheered by the spectators. This time it took a full minute for the judge to quieten the court. The judge looked at the signalman sourly. "Mr Meakin, you cannot expect this court to have any sympathy with you. Simply tell us what happened – we are not interested in how you *felt*."

Meakin closed his eyes. "The carriages were lit by gas, of course. The gas cylinders exploded. They set fire to the wood of the coaches. The men that were still alive were trapped in the flames. We ran down to help. But we couldn't do that much. I tried to help one man. His leg was caught. I tried to pull him free but the flames were getting nearer. Then he looked at the soldier next to me and he called out to him, 'Shoot me mate! Please! Please, for God's sake shoot me!'"

Someone in the gallery sobbed. "I think we've heard enough, Mr Meakin," the judge said. He put down his pen and folded his hands on the bench in front of him. "You have pleaded guilty to the charge of manslaughter. You are to blame for the deaths of 227 people and injury to a further 246. You, Tinsley, were the man on duty at the time. You must bear most of the blame for this tragedy. I sentence you to three years in prison."

There was a groan from the gallery. "Not enough!" someone said. James Tinsley's head drooped and his thin shoulders sagged.

"George Meakin," the judge went on coldly. "You assisted Tinsley in breaking the rules of the Caledonian Railway Company. Rules put there to protect the public. I sentence you to 18 months in prison."

The judge rose to his feet and left the court in a swirl of scarlet, red as blood or fire ... or a signal that says "Stop. Danger."

James Tinsley said, "I forgot all about the local train." But he was never able to explain just how you can step off a train and immediately forget it is there! The two signalmen were horrified by what they had done; they didn't need the judge to tell them they were guilty. They were haunted by the sights they had seen that day, by the screams of the dying and the horrors that the soldiers suffered. There were stories of men having trapped limbs cut off to free them from wreckage before the fire reached them – one officer is said to have drawn his sword and cut his own arm off. Tinsley and Meakin went to prison but their mental health was destroyed. Both left prison after a year, broken men left to suffer a life-sentence of guilt.

The unfortunate thing about Quintinshill is that almost everyone survived the first crash. It was when the second express ploughed into the wreckage that there was a huge loss of life. A similar thing happened at Mikawashima station near Tokyo in Japan. In May 1962 a goods train hit a passenger train; as the passengers climbed to safety a third train hit them. Many of the people who had survived the first crash were killed in the second crash. That is cruel luck. One hundred and sixty-three people died and more than 300 were injured.

F
A
C
T

O
F
I
L
E

Railway Disasters

1. **Siberian disaster, Russia, 1989.** In 1989 Russia suffered even worse luck. A gas pipeline exploded in open countryside. No one should have been hurt. But a train was passing close by and it was blown off the rails. Still the people on board could have escaped with few injuries, but another train was passing in the opposite direction so the first train was knocked into the path of the second train. Three events happening at the same time made for a major disaster. But the bad luck didn't end there for the passengers. The coaches, like those at Quintinshill, were made of wood and caught fire immediately. Passengers who survived the blast, the derailment and the head-on crash fell victim to the flames. Four hundred died, half of them children, and 700 more were injured.

2. **Tay Bridge disaster, Scotland, 1879.** One of the most spectacular rail crashes in history was on the other side of Scotland from Quintinshill. In December 1879 a train was crossing the Tay Bridge in a storm when the bridge collapsed. Seventy-nine passengers were catapulted into the dark, icy waters of the Tay below. There were no survivors at all. The bridge was unsafe and the bridge inspector was questioned. It turned out that he had no qualifications and no experience. He wouldn't have spotted a faulty bridge if it had fallen on his head.

F
A
C
T
O
F
I
L
E

3. **The Chatsworth wreck, USA, 1887.** In America a wooden bridge was weakened when it caught fire. But the fire was started by railway workers who had been burning weeds by the side of the track. A driver saw the fire but he was too late to stop his train. The weight of the train on the burning supports made them give way. Eighty-two people died as coaches crashed into the ravine below.

4. **The Mondane Hill crash, France, 1917.** The Quintinshill soldiers were on their way to fight in the First World War. Survivors said the scenes at the crash were worse than any they saw in battle. But in 1917 French soldiers suffered a worse disaster. More than 1,000 French troops were going home for Christmas and their train was overloaded. Half of them would be dead before the train reached its destination. The driver warned the railway company that the old handbrakes on the carriage wouldn't hold them on a steep hill at Mondane. His managers told him to drive it anyway. The driver was proved right. The train picked up speed as it ran down the hill and the brakes failed to hold it. The rushing locomotive managed to take the sharp bend at the bottom of the hill but the carriages behind it went straight ahead. The wooden carriages caught fire as they had at Quintinshill two years before. But this time the soldiers were carrying live ammunition, and this began to explode in the flames, making the situation far worse.

5. **Germany, 1998.** Modern trains and signals are much safer than they were in the days of the Quintinshill disaster. But the trains travel much faster so the disasters can be horrific when they do happen. In June 1998 a German train was travelling at over 120 miles an hour when a wheel broke and jumped off the track. In the next minute the train travelled two miles, dragging the derailed coach until it tried to pass under a road bridge. The carriage smashed into the road bridge and brought it crashing down on to the coaches. Almost 100 people died. Within a month a wheel broke on a British high-speed train near London – no one was hurt because the driver stopped before it reached a bridge or a passing train. The difference between death and survival can sometimes be simple luck.

6. **The *Rocket* accident, Liverpool, England, 1829.** Some people have always been frightened by the idea of rail travel. When they heard that trains would travel at over 40 miles an hour they said that passengers, in open coaches, would have the air sucked from their lungs and die! The first railway accidents in 1828 were caused by exploding boilers, but the most famous early victim was a guest at a railway contest to find the fastest locomotive in Britain. A witness described the unfortunate death:

The Northumbrian *locomotive pulled a carriage containing the Duke of Wellington. When it stopped the Right Honourable William Huskisson MP stepped down on to the track along which the* Rocket *was seen rapidly coming up. The Duke of Wellington stretched out to shake the hand of Huskisson.*

A hurried, friendly grasp was given and, before it was loosed, there was a general cry of "Get in! Get in!" Mr Huskisson, flustered, attempted to get around the open door but in so doing was struck down by the Rocket. *His first words on being raised were, "I have met my death!"*

He died later that night.

The *Rocket* went on to win the speed trials at an amazing top speed of 36 m.p.h.

7. **Whangaehu Bridge train crash, New Zealand, 1953.** In New Zealand on Christmas Eve 1953, a postmaster noticed that the river Whangaehu was unusually swollen. The rail bridge was under water and the Auckland express was due. He ran down the track, waving to the driver – but he was too late. The weight of the train on the flooded bridge caused it to collapse and the locomotive dragged the front carriages into the river. Passengers from the rear carriages bravely formed a human chain to pull survivors out. But it was another sort of chain – a chain of events – that had led to the disaster. There was a lake in the crater of the nearby Ruapehu volcano. The volcano erupted, spewed out the lake water along with rocks and lava into the river Whangaehu. The river flooded and the rush of mud-thick water weakened the bridge. The disaster was made worse by the train being crowded with people going home for Christmas. The death toll rached 131 and a further 20 people were never found. The luckiest survivor was probably the woman washed 300 metres from the crash, buried up to her neck in freezing mud with just one arm free. She was dug out, badly injured, and survived.

8. Galleria delle Armi tunnel disaster, Italy 1944. Not all rail disasters have been the result of crashes. In March 1944 an express train entered a long tunnel at Galleria delle Armi in Italy. The locomotive wheels began to skid on the rails and the train ground to a halt. The driver could have reversed out. Instead he ordered the coal fires to be stoked up for more power. The tunnel filled with smoke and the passengers were suffocated in their sleep. Five hundred and twenty died, only five lived.

UNDER THE GROUND

Coal-mines are dangerous places. You are working under millions of tonnes of earth that can collapse and crush you. You rely on pumps to bring fresh air in and to push out the poison gases that can explode or suffocate you silently. You depend on water pumps to keep your narrow workplace free of freezing black floods. And you rely on luck. Luck was something the men and boys at Hartley Colliery in northern England lacked.

The Hartley pit disaster, Northumberland, January 1862

The cat was dead. The tall, grey-haired man carried it across the snow-speckled yard towards the long, low wooden hut.

The eyes of 50 women and children watched him. They stood around the orange glow of the brazier. It melted the flecks of snow on their black shawls but they didn't seem to notice the cold. Snow blew over their thin shoes but they didn't move their feet.

He saw them watching and flicked a wrist to send the cat tumbling into a pile of coal dust.

The man opened the door of the hut and amber candlelight spilled over the yard. He turned. "If you would care to come into the hut I will tell you what progress we've made."

"They're dead, aren't they?" one of the women cried.

"If you will come into the hut, please," he said and turned away from her fierce, hot gaze.

The women and children moved slowly at first then with more urgency. They whispered to the frozen children and shooed them into the bleak wooden hut. There were benches facing a platform. The man stood on the platform, head lowered, afraid to meet their curious looks. A second man with bandaged hands and head sat on a chair and looked at them with a strange expression of love and pity.

At last, the women and children were seated and silent. The standing man cleared his throat and looked over the heads of the gathering, not daring to meet one of the 50 pairs of eyes that looked back. He nodded towards the man in the chair. "You all know Thomas Watson here. He was there when the accident happened. He's come from the hospital to explain what it was like down there. And, for those of you who don't know me, I'm William Coulson. I am the engineer that sank the Hartley mine shaft and it's me that's been put in charge of the rescue."

"Tell us about the cat!" the fierce-eyed woman cried.

Thomas Watson whispered a few words to William Coulson. "You are Mrs Sarah Bewick?" Coulson asked.

"Aye. What of it?"

"Please, Mrs Bewick, let Thomas Watson here tell his tale."

The woman folded her arms and her lips closed in an almost invisible line. Someone gave a sob but it was quickly muffled. Thomas Watson spread his bandaged hands. "Neighbours," he began. "We've been unlucky. The accident happened just before eleven o'clock. At that time the men who were starting work had gone down the shaft but the men finishing work hadn't come up to the surface. At any other time there'd be a hundred men in the pit. At eleven yesterday morning there were two hundred."

"Two hundred and four," Sarah Bewick said in a flat voice. "Including my Jim."

"I was one of the first to take the lift up towards the surface," Thomas Watson went on. "We were near the top when there was a tremendous crash. The cage of the lift was smashed and young George Sharp and Jim's brother Robert were thrown out. You know by now what caused the crash. The massive steel arm of the water pump that hangs over the shaft. It snapped and fell down the shaft – twenty tons of it. That was our next bit of bad luck."

"It should never have snapped!" a thin, old woman cried.

"Aye, Maggie! You tell him!" someone cheered.

"It wasn't bad luck. It was bad workmanship!"

William Coulson, the engineer, raised a hand. "That will all be looked into at the proper time."

"But that was the only way in and out of the pit!" Sarah Bewick said fiercely. "When that shaft gets blocked the men below are trapped. Any sensible engineer builds a pit with *two* shafts! You can't trust to luck that the one shaft won't be shut off!"

"Aye!" the women cheered.

"It was a question of cost," Coulson said, wringing his hands. "But that will be looked into when there's an inquiry. Meanwhile you should listen to this brave man's story."

The women went silent again and looked at Thomas Watson. "I was in the cage with George Sharp's father and we could hear his son crying out from below. The broken arm had smashed the lift then jammed in the shaft and brought down tons of rubble. George and Robert were half buried by it. The other two hundred men were underneath it. The rescuers lowered ropes and they pulled me up."

William Coulson rested a hand on Watson's shoulder. "He's not telling you the full story!" he said. "Thomas Watson here had no light because water was streaming down the shaft and soaking the lamps. But he found the lift rope and climbed down it in the darkness till he reached George and Robert. He put his own life in danger just to help those two comrades."

Watson lowered his head and said quietly, "We prayed together. We sang hymns. I couldn't free their bodies but I know their souls were light when they died."

The women on the benches moaned, some sobbed and one muttered, "Amen."

"Thomas was in that dark shaft for eleven hours before the rescuers reached him with a rope," Coulson explained. "Old

Sharp had been too weak to cling to the rope. He slipped and fell back down the shaft. He must have died next to his son."

"The water was pouring on to my head," Watson said, taking up the story. "I found a small hollow in the side of the shaft to shelter in. I heard stones falling. I heard rescuers calling but I was so weak I didn't know which way was forward or which way was up to the surface." Suddenly the man looked up and let his eyes meet every gaze that was fixed on him. "Then ... when I was at my weakest and most hopeless ... I prayed. I shut my eyes tight and I prayed. I've not long been a Christian but I said every prayer I knew and a few I made up for myself. I prayed for your men, your fathers and children that I knew were trapped below me."

Watson stopped. He shook his bandaged head in wonder and spread his hands. "Then, when I opened my eyes, I saw a blaze of golden light. And in the light I saw the loop of rope from the top of the shaft. I grasped it and pulled. The men at the top hauled me up and I was saved. God heard my prayers and answered them. He will answer yours!"

"Can God lift the beam that is blocking the shaft?" Sarah Bewick said bitterly.

Watson closed his eyes. "No, Sarah. No. But ... I saw that light, that impossible light. God is there – and he can bring your man to the safety of his heaven."

"I'd rather have him in the safety of my hearth," she said.

Coulson stepped forward. "We have been trying to dig past the broken beam, as you know. Men have been coming from all over the country to help with this rescue."

"There's more come sightseeing!" Old Maggie spat. "You can't move in the tavern for visitors come to see the disaster! It's like a seaside trip for them town folks. If they'd set their hands to the digging our men would have been out twenty hours ago!"

There was an angry rumble of agreement from the women.

"The police are keeping them out of the pit yard," Coulson said. "Now don't give up hope, Mrs Bewick. Your men will have plenty of water down there."

"You stopped digging last night," she accused.

"The more we dug the more the walls collapsed into the shaft. We had to stop to line the sides with wooden panels," he replied. "But we started again this evening. We should be through in two hours – four at the most!"

She raised one eyebrow. "We saw the cat," she said.

A baby whimpered. There was a soft creak as the door opened. The orange light of the candles flickered in the north wind and snowflakes flew through the door. A man blackened by coal stood there.

He looked at Coulson. The shake of the newcomer's head was so slight that most people would have missed it.

"Come in, Mr Dunn!" Coulson called to the stranger. He was relieved that someone had come to share the burden of the women's anger. "This is Mr Matthias Dunn – District Inspector."

Dunn walked slowly to the platform and stood in front of it. His eyes were red-rimmed with tiredness and, for all his strength, there were white tracks of tears on his coal-dusted face. His deep voice cracked as he spoke. "Aye. The cat. The men we sent down this afternoon came up sick and dizzy. We lowered the cat down in a basket. Ten minutes later we hauled it up and the cat was dead."

"Say it man!" Maggie groaned.

At first the word refused to come. It stuck in his throat. At last he said it. "Gas. The shaft is filled with rising gas. I'm sorry. If the shaft is filled with it then it's like as not the pit below is filled. I'm sorry."

"But you heard rapping noises just this afternoon!" Sarah Bewick argued.

"Small stones falling down the shaft. The last real rapping we heard was two days ago now. I'm sorry. We'll have to stop digging. There's no point risking the lives of the rescuers..." Dunn's voice tailed off.

"Not when our men are already dead," Sarah Bewick said.

"I'm sorry," Dunn repeated.

The women rose, some clutching babies, others leading hollow-cheeked children by the hand. They left the hut and made their way home to prepare for the funerals.

The three men were left in the dim orange candle-glow. "Two hundred and four men and boys," Coulson sighed. "I feel so sorry for them."

Watson rose to his feet, shaking his head. "No, Mr Coulson. The gas is a gentle way to go. The dead are with their maker in a place where there's no back-breaking work, no damp, no lightless holes. It's the ones that are left that need our pity now."

Seven days after the Hartley shaft was blocked the first rescuers broke through at 11:00 a.m. It seemed that the men below ground had tried to dig their way out. They didn't know that the blockage was ten metres thick or that the solid steel beam of 20 tonnes lay in their way.

At 2:00 p.m. that day a telegram arrived at Hartley from Queen Victoria. It stated:

"The Queen is most anxious to hear that there are hopes of saving the poor people in the colliery, for whom her heart bleeds."

The Queen would be disappointed.

At 4:00 p.m. the same day, the first of the trapped men were discovered. Dead.

Five days later the bodies were raised to the surface for the largest mass burial ever held outside of a war. The oldest was 71 and the youngest was just ten years old. Sixty-thousand people lined the road from Hartley to the churchyard.

In one cottage there were seven men and children lost. Four hundred and seven women, children and old people were left without anyone to earn their income. A fund was set up that raised the vast sum of £82,000 in just over a year.

The rescuers were given silver medals – William Coulson was given a gold one. The greatest effect was that the law was

31

changed. After Hartley, the law insisted that all pits should have two shafts so that if one was blocked the miners still had an escape route.

Some of the trapped men managed to write messages before they died. Jim Bewick had no pencil or paper but managed to scratch his farewell message on his tool box:

FRIDAY AFTERNOON
MY DEAREST SARAH - I LEAVE YOU

Mine Disasters

The Hartley deaths could have been prevented if there had been a second entrance to the mine. Many disasters could have been avoided if more care had been taken. It's easy to look back and say what *should* have been done, but sometimes disasters were needed before the lessons were learned. The main dangers were...

1. **Gas poisoning**. Most mines suffer problems with underground gas. It poisons the air and kills the miners or it explodes. But the gas has no colour and no smell. A test for gas was to take a canary down the mine – if the canary fell off its perch, it was probably gassed and the miners would stop work. A furnace at the bottom of a mine shaft would be used to suck in fresh air but these didn't always work.

The draft of fresh air sometimes chilled the bare-backed miners so they deliberately built wooden shields to keep the draughts off their backs. Without the fresh air they could be poisoned if they broke through to a pocket of gas.

F
A
C
T

O

F
I
L
E

2. **Gas explosion.** Candles that early miners used would often spark off a deadly explosion. In the 1820s "Safety Lamps" were invented.

But in Blantyre, near Glasgow, in 1877 miners were still using open oil lamps in a very gassy mine. Gas flashes happened all the time and the miners simply threw themselves on their faces while the flame rushed over their heads. In the same mine they used explosives to blast rock out of the way. It's probable that one of these explosions set off a gas flash that killed over 200 men in Blantyre that year.

Still men risked their lives taking pipes and matches down the mine for a smoke, even though they were banned. In 1879, 28 more men died in Blantyre and partly-smoked pipes were found on the bodies.

Electric lighting should have made the mines safer, but sparks from loose wires were every bit as deadly as the old candles had been. Electric sparks were blamed for Britain's worst mining disaster when 440 men died at Senghenydd in South Wales.

3. **Flooding.** Miners expect to find water as they dig below the surface. They have invented many types of water scoops, drains and pumps to keep their working areas dry. But as soon as a mine is abandoned it can quickly fill with water. That is not a problem normally. But underground workers coming from *another* direction may break through into the old mine. The flood of water bursting in would be so sudden and so great that no pump or drain in the world could cope with it. The miners underground at the time will drown.

The answer is obvious. Every mine should have careful plans drawn. When the mine closes, everyone can look at the plans and new mines can keep away from the dangerously

water-filled old mines. But that hasn't always happened.

In 1925 at Newcastle's Montagu Pit 38 miners drowned when they broke through to the abandoned Paradise Pit. The plans showed the old pit clearly – but no one had passed on the plans to the company digging the new mine.

4. Accidents. Explosions are rare but spectacular disasters. More deaths have happened from everyday accidents. Mines are dangerous places, with ropes that snap and wheels that crush and machines that slip and rocks that fall. But one of the saddest disasters happened because of the waste dug out of a Welsh pit. It was piled into a small mountain on a hillside above the school in Aberfan. In 1966 two million tonnes of the black sludge slipped and buried the school below it. One hundred and sixteen children were crushed or drowned within minutes.

There had been a warning three years earlier when a small slide had happened. The people in charge took little notice. Again it needed a major disaster before the lesson was learnt.

At Hartley Colliery sightseers crowded the local tavern, at Blantyre they packed drunkenly into trains to see the spectacle. At Aberfan the news spread even quicker because of radio and television news. The roads to the disaster site were so crowded with these heartless ghouls that rescue vehicles could not get through to help.

Sometimes disasters bring out the best in people. At the same time they bring out the worst in others.

BEYOND THE FLAMES

*P*ride is a deadly sin they say, and sins are punished. So when the Titanic was proudly named "unsinkable" it sank. And in Chicago in 1903 the Iroquois Theatre was advertised as being "absolutely fireproof". There was only one real result of a proud boast like that, wasn't there?

The Iroquois Theatre disaster, Chicago, December 1903

The woman inside the glass box office had bright eyes that glittered greedily in the yellow glow of the gaslights. She faced the woman and two children and explained slyly, "The theatre is full, madam. This show has come all the way over from Drury Lane in London, England, and we're sold out till well into the New Year."

The older child, a girl with a thick, dark pigtail looked disappointed; the little boy at her side was just bewildered. "Want to see Mr Bluebeard," he said in a thin, piping voice.

"He'll be so disappointed," his mother sighed and began to turn away.

"But I may be able to squeeze those two little ones in," the ticketseller said quickly. "It'll cost you a dollar each and they'll have to stand!"

"A dollar each! Just to stand?" the woman said and began to walk away.

But the little boy said, "When we going to see Mr Bluebeard?"

His mother sighed and muttered to the girl, "It's robbery."

"Jim'll be so upset if we don't get in," the girl said quietly. "We've been promising him this since Christmas."

"I know, Lizzie, I know," her mother sighed. She took two coins from her purse and pressed them into the girl's hand.

"There's not enough for candy in the interval."

"That's all right," the girl said. "I've brought a couple of oranges and a handful of nuts left over from Christmas. Thanks, Ma!"

"You look after Jim. You look after him!"

"He'll be all right with me, Ma," Lizzie promised. She took the two dollars and waved goodbye to her mother. The woman at the cash desk snatched the money from the girl's hand. The girl waited. "Do I get a ticket?" she asked.

"You don't have a seat so you don't get a ticket," the woman told her and slipped the two dollars into her pocket. "Just squeeze yourselves in at the back."

As Lizzie and Jim entered the theatre the lights were dimming. The roar of the excited audience was subsiding and the curtain was rising. The crush was so great that the two children couldn't see the stage. It was hot and the air smelled stale but little Jim was awed by the magic. "Where's Mr Bluebeard?" he asked.

Music filled the theatre from the orchestra in front of the stage and the air trembled as 2,000 people stamped and clapped. At last the children who crowded into the aisles began to sit on the floor and Lizzie and Jim could see the distant stage. There were dancers in brilliant costumes in a rainbow of colours leaping across the stage. Lizzie turned to look at her little brother. She wanted to see the golden stage light reflected in his excited eyes. What she saw was a cross frown. "So where's Mr Bluebeard?" he asked.

Mr Bluebeard was in a dressing-room behind the stage. "Ye gods!" he was groaning as he felt the theatre shake to the drumming of 2,000 pairs of feet. "I hate kids!"

The actor, Charles Gainsborough, daubed on bright greasepaint then turned to his dresser, who was holding out his coat. "They make you a good living," the dresser sniffed.

Gainsborough fixed the dresser with a haughty stare that he used on stage – the Bluebeard stare he called it – and said, "It is just money, Hank. I'm not interested in money! I am interested in Art!" He threw his hands in the air as he did when his wicked Bluebeard character was captured at the end. "Last year I was playing Shakespeare!"

"And Shakespeare lost," the dresser grumbled.

There was a knock on the dressing-room door. "Your cue, Mr Gainsborough!" Hank said.

The actor shrugged himself into the golden coat and sighed. "Once more unto the breach, dear friends!" he cried and swept out of the dressing room. He pushed through the crowded corridors, where 400 performers and stagehands were hurrying about their business. He reached the side of the stage just in time to hear the crashing chords of music that signalled his entrance.

When Charles Gainsborough strode on to the stage the theatre trembled with the roar of anger and joy. Little Jim's voice was lost. "Nasty Mr Bluebeard!" he screamed.

The bored actor waited until the noise had died a little so he could begin to speak. "My name is Bluebeard – the most handsome man in France!" he managed to say before his voice was drowned by the howling audience.

Charles Gainsborough was fighting a losing battle against 2,000 excited people. He hurried through his opening scene and marched off.

A fresh canvas screen was lowered on to the stage to show a woodland scene. The audience calmed a little as 16 singers entered. The yellow light faded and a blue electric arc light lit the performers.

"What's happening?" Jim asked. "Where's Mr Bluebeard gone?"

"Back to his castle," Lizzie said. "Now hush and watch!"

"Why's it gone dark?" the boy went on.

"It's night."

"What's that light?"

"Moonlight," Lizzie sighed. "Now shush and listen!"

The singers started to sing a gentle "In the Pale Moonlight" while the audience grew a little restless and began to unwrap candy bars with a loud crackling of papers.

There was a sharp crack that few in the audience noticed, but the main blue arc light seemed to have disappeared and left the stage lit only by a pale yellow wash.

No one realized that the Iroquois Theatre disaster had started.

At the side of the stage Charles Gainsborough hissed, "What's happened?"

Hank was holding the cloak the actor needed for the next

41

scene. "The main arc light's blown," he said.

Gainsborough growled. "I need that light for my big scene in the castle. I hope they can fix it in the interval."

The dresser looked up to the girders high above the stage. They held the electric lights and the oil-painted canvas sheets that would be dropped each time there was a scene change. They were held in place by a maze of ropes like some great sailing ship. The dresser peered up to the broken arc light and saw a yellow flicker. "No chance, Mr Gainsborough!"

The actor looked up and groaned. "It's caught fire." He turned to a stage hand. "Deal with that burning lamp!"

The stagehand snatched a fire extinguisher – no more than a can of powder – and began to climb a ladder up to the roof of the stage. By the time he reached the lamp the flame had set light to a curtain. The stagehand threw the powder and flapped a hand at the growing gold of the flame.

"This could stop the performance!" the actor hissed. He grabbed a passing stagehand. "Sound the fire alarm."

"There isn't one, sir," the man said.

"Then run along and call the fire brigade!"

The man looked up, saw the flame leap across to an oil-painted canvas and begin to flower into a golden star of fire. He ran.

On stage the singers finished their song and the audience clapped politely but without much enthusiasm. As they left the stage the lights were dimmed for the next scene change. It was in the dimness that the glow of the spreading fire could be seen from the audience.

"Fire!" someone in the front row cried.

The first move of the audience was forward. They wanted to see if it was true. When the cry spread they began to back away. The seats were arranged in long rows. Those in the middle of the rows could see no way out so they started to climb over the backs of their seats. The people who were standing in the aisles found it hard to turn in the crush and make their way towards the back of the theatre.

Lizzie saw the dark surge of bodies silhouetted by the yellow glow. She snatched for her brother's small hand and dragged it through the door at the back of the theatre. She was one of the lucky ones. Last in was first out. "Let's get right out of here!" she gasped and dragged at the tiny hand, pulling the child past the box office and towards the street.

"Let go!" the child screamed.

Lizzie turned. The hand she held belonged to a little fair-haired girl. Children were bursting out of the narrow doorways but Jim was nowhere in sight.

"Lower the safety curtain!" Charles Gainsborough screamed to the stage manager. Then he ran on to the stage. "There's no need to panic!" he shouted at the backs of the retreating audience.

They stopped for a moment and looked at the man they thought of as Bluebeard. The greasepaint was trickling down his face as it mingled with sweat. One or two children booed him.

"Listen! The safety curtain will come down!" he cried and pointed. Sure enough the heavy, flame-proof curtain was slowly lowered to the stage. "The fire will be contained backstage. There will be plenty of time for you to get out safely. Don't panic."

For a few moments the words seemed to work. Gainsborough turned to the stage manager. "For God's sake don't open any backstage doors till that curtain's down. The draught would feed the flames."

The stage manager shook his head. "Mister Gainsborough, there are four hundred people back here. How do I stop them?"

There was a gasp from the audience. The actor turned back to them. They were looking past him at the safety curtain. It had stopped moving. Gainsborough ran back and looked up at it. The curtain was caught on a steel cable. Stagehands tugged at it frantically. Someone took a saw and began to cut at it but it was too little and soon it was too late.

The cast of the play saw the fire racing over the oiled canvases and thin curtains. Someone pushed at the loading-bay doors at the back of the stage and let in a gale of air to feed the fire. The dull yellow flames burst into a brilliant white tongue of fire that was swept under the safety curtain and rolled towards the audience.

The tangle of ropes burned through and the painted scenery crashed on to the stage, an oil-soaked bonfire.

"Don't panic!" Gainsborough cried. This time no one heard him.

At the front door Lizzie tried to find a way back into the theatre. But a woman stumbled and fell. Ten people seemed to trample over her in a second, then more fell over her only to be trampled in their turn. The door was blacked by fallen bodies. Wide-eyed, wide-mouthed screaming adults and children were hurling themselves for the little daylight they could see over the heap of crushed bodies. Lizzie was pushed back and back.

A fireman brushed past her and tugged her out of the way. "No way through here!" he called to his colleagues. "Let's try the stage door!"

"My brother!" Lizzie cried, but no one heard her.

She was forced out into the middle of the road where taxis and buses and cars and horse-drawn vehicles stopped and blocked the way. The girl didn't notice the cold December wind. She wiped the mixture of sleet and tears from her eyes and scoured the mass of sobbing, gasping, wailing people for the sight of one little boy.

She was pushed aside and found herself forced to the corner

of the building. The side alley there led to the stage door. Actors in their brilliant costumes spilled out into the alley and were pushed roughly aside by firefighters.

A tall man dressed in a flame-yellow coat walked towards her in a daze. His face was a hideous mess of running greasepaint and soot. He clutched a small bundle in his arms. A child dressed in a rough brown tweed coat.

The child turned his head slowly and looked at Lizzie.

"Nasty Mr Bluebeard, Lizzie. Nasty Mr Bluebeard."

Tears stung Lizzie's eyes as she reached up and gently took her brother from the arms of the actor. The man sniffed back his own tears. "He ... he ran towards me. Everyone else was crushed to the back of the theatre. This kid ran towards me waving his little fist!"

"Nasty Mr Bluebeard!" Jim said.

"He doesn't understand!" Charles Gainsborough moaned.

Lizzie buried her brother's face in her neck. The nightmare would never leave her if she lived to be 100. "I pray he never understands," she said. She took a deep breath and tried to speak calmly to little Jim. "Say thank you to Mr Bluebeard."

The boy turned his face towards the actor and scowled. "Nasty Mr Bluebeard," he said.

There were 30 exits at the Iroquois Theatre but few of them were marked. Some had heavy curtains across them and some were locked. The theatre with just 1,600 seats had about 2,000 people in it at the time of the fire.

Very few were burned to death. About 200 were suffocated by the smoke, but the greatest number of the victims – 400 – were trampled in the crush to get out. They were found in the tangled mass of bodies with boot marks on their faces, with clothes ripped from their bodies and even with flesh ripped from their bones.

The 400 performers all escaped.

Greed played its part as it often does. Fire-safety inspectors had been "bought off" with free theatre tickets. Undertakers raised their prices for the funerals.

Theatres were checked for safety throughout the USA and 50 were closed. New laws were passed to make sure this sort of disaster could never happen again in an American theatre. A familiar story.

Fire Disasters

1. **The Great Fire of London, 1666.** Not all disasters are as terrible as they seem. John Farynor, a baker in Pudding Lane, went to bed without damping down his ovens properly. His shop caught fire and within three days that small fire had spread to destroy 87 churches and 13,000 homes. But only eight people died in the huge fire and in fact, the Great Fire of London may have saved far more lives than it took. For it burned down the dreadful slums and killed many of the rats that had brought the Great Plague to the city the year before. London rebuilt was a healthier city.

2. **The Great Chicago fire, 1871.** A cow became the most famous animal in Chicago's history. Mrs O'Leary's cow was being milked when it lashed out with a back leg and kicked over a paraffin lamp. The straw caught fire and then the barn and then the house – and eventually the city. Mrs O'Leary always denied she was to blame. Her drunken lodger Dennis Sullivan was also suspected. It's thought he crept into the barn for a drink and a smoke – a spark from his pipe started the fire. Dennis also refused to take the blame. He said he was across the road when he saw the flames. He ran into the barn to save a calf – his wooden leg got stuck in a crack in the floor and he had to take it off to escape; he hopped out clinging to the neck of the rescued calf. Believe either or neither. The result was that 250 people died and there was 200 million dollars worth of damage. An expensive cow! But out of the ashes a safer and finer city grew, just as it had in London.

3. **The Boston Coconut Grove fire, 1942.** The fire in the Coconut Grove nightclub was smaller than the Fire of London but killed far more. It was started just as carelessly. A customer took a light bulb out of its socket so his corner of the room would be comfortably dim. A young waiter went to put a light bulb back in. He lit a match to see where the socket was but the flame set alight one of the papier-mâché imitation palm trees. Fire spread quickly across the room with more palm leaves, silk curtains and plastic furniture to feed it. The main exit was a revolving door – hopelessly slow and a death-trap. When firemen finally broke it down they found bodies piled six-deep behind it. A naval officer tried to keep people calm and organized – he was found dead with the uniform ripped from his back. Emergency doors had been bolted shut and others were hidden behind curtains. Half of the 900 people in the club died that night.

F

A

C

T

TITANIC
RMS · RMS
TITANIC

O

F

I

L

E

4. The Cinq-Sept club fire, St Laurent du Pont, France, 1970.
American nightclubs improved their safety after the Coconut
Grove fire but it seems other countries didn't learn from the
tragic lesson. On 1 November 1970 the pop group Storm were
playing at the Cinq-Sept club and young people were frantic to
see them. There was just one entrance, through a turnstile
almost three metres high. To stop anyone breaking in all the
emergency doors were locked. Plastic sheets were hung to
decorate the hall and it was packed with 200 fans. At 1:40
a.m. a young man dropped a match on a cushion that caught
fire and was soon shooting flames up towards the plastic
sheets. In just 30 seconds the hall was ablaze and the fumes
from the burning plastic were black and poisonous. Nearly 150
people died almost instantly. Some headed for the exit but the
turnstile jammed when only 30 had got through. The fire
services were delayed because, like the Iroquois Theatre
disaster, there was no contact with the fire station – there was
not even a telephone in the club so someone had to drive over
a kilometre while people died. In less than 10 hours the roads
to St Laurent du Pont were jammed with traffic as sightseers
flocked to the area.

5. The São Paulo office fire, Brazil, 1974. You would imagine
that a tall block of offices would have fire-escapes, but the 25-
storey Joelma Building in São Paolo had hardly any. If there
was a fire on one floor then the people above it would be
trapped. To make things worse, the building was built from
inflammable materials and the local fire brigade hadn't the
equipment to fight fires much above the height of a house –
their ladders were simply too short! So, when a fire broke out
on the eleventh floor, it was bound to be disastrous. Victims
preferred to jump to their deaths rather than wait for the

flames to swallow them. One man plunged down crying, "Goodbye! Goodbye!" Sightseers arrived to watch and abandoned more than 300,000 cars so ambulances couldn't get in to help the injured. One daring fireman swung from a rope attached to a nearby building. He rescued 18 people that way though he was almost killed when a man jumped from a higher window and collided with him.

6. San Francisco, 1906. When an earthquake rocked San Francisco in 1906 there were many people crushed in the crumbling buildings. But the problems for the city didn't end when the shock waves died down. Ovens and fires that had been knocked over set fire to the buildings, broken electric cables sparked and cracked gas pipes flared. There were over 50 fires around the city and the fire department had just 38 horse-drawn fire engines to fight them. The earthquake had smashed every main water pipe so there was no water to pour on the fires.

Some people survived the earthquake and were trapped alive in the rubble only to be burned to death when the fires started – 80 died in one hotel that way. It is reckoned that the

FACTOFILE

fire destroyed 20 times as much as the earthquake. One of the real horrors was that when homeless people began stealing from shattered stores the mayor of San Francisco said that the army was to shoot anyone committing a crime at the time of the disaster. It is cruel when you've survived an earthquake *and* a fire only to be shot as you try to scavenge a little food for your family!

7. Tokyo, 1923. The story in Tokyo was similar to that of San Francisco 17 years before. But the fires that raged after the earthquake were worse. People rushed to the parks to escape the burning buildings and even stood up to their necks in the water of the canals. One woman stood all day with her baby on her head and survived this way. Others were later found dead with their bodies preserved but their heads charred. Whirlwinds of flame formed and swept over the city, snatching people into the air and dropping burned remains miles away. Parents searching for children held out their names on pieces of paper because the scorching air had dried their throats and left them speechless. The nearby port of Yokohama was affected the same way. People ran to the sea for protection but saw that oil tanks had been burst and the sea was a sheet of flames. A quarter of a million people were killed or severely injured in the cities.

8. Australia, 1983. A long drought in south-eastern Australia dried the bush and gale-force winds whipped a series of small fires into a furnace spread over thousands of square miles. Some fires were started when power lines were blown down and sparked amongst the tinder-dry grass. Other fires were certainly started deliberately by maniacs who wanted the excitement of a major disaster on their doorstep. A fireman

F
A
C
T
O
F
I
L
E

said the flames advanced towards the towns "like an express train". Nothing the fire service could do would stop it. Only rain helped put an end to the fire that had destroyed 2,000 homes and killed 74 people. The fires started on 16 February ... which just happened to be "Ash Wednesday".

FROM THE
LAND OF THE GREEN

People change. There was a terrible famine in Ethiopia in 1984–85 when 10 million people were starving and a million died. Many of the richer nations raised money to help them then and whenever famine strikes around the world they are still willing to give. But it hasn't always been that way. In the past the rich have turned their backs on the poor and hungry, and left them to die or to try and help themselves.

The Irish Famine, 1845-50

"Have you ever eaten anybody, Ma?" the boy asked.

He had red hair and eyes as green as the sea he was sailing over. The coast of Ireland was fading into a moss-coloured smudge on the horizon behind them as they sailed towards the setting sun.

"What a thing to ask!" his mother cried.

"Michael Mulloy's eaten somebody. He had them in a soup his grandma cooked and he said it tasted just like chicken."

"It probably was a chicken, Seamus. You don't want to go believing everything Michael Mulloy tells you. He's a terrible liar!"

"So he hasn't eaten anybody?"

"No!"

"And you haven't, Ma?"

"No ... though I'll nibble that tongue out of your head if you don't stop going on about eating people and asking silly questions!"

The boy looked at the deck where they were sitting and chewed slowly on a piece of hard bread. He found if he ate slowly he could make food last longer. He couldn't remember a time when he hadn't been hungry. He turned to his father.

"What are you reading, Da?"

"A newspaper."

Seamus raised his stick-thin arm and punched his father on the arm. "I know *that*, Da. I mean what are you reading about?"

"Always the curious one," Mr O'Leary grinned. His teeth were crooked and loose in his raw gums, but he'd been a handsome man once.

"What are you reading about?" Seamus persisted.

"I'm reading about an Englishman..."

"I don't like Englishmen. Michael Mulloy says they're evil and he'd eat one if he ever met one," the green-eyed boy said.

"Well, this Englishman's a lord. Lord John Russell. He was speaking in the English Parliament and he was talking about Ireland," Mr O'Leary said patiently.

"Tell us what he said, Da!"

The man squinted at the small print with eyes a more faded green than his son's. He read the statement in a mock-English accent. " 'We have made Ireland the most degraded and miserable country in the world. All the world is crying shame upon us but we are ignoring the disgrace and the results of our misrule.' "

"But what does it mean, Da?"

The man steadied himself as the ship rolled in the Atlantic waters and its tired old timbers creaked.

"It means the English are ashamed of what they've done to us," Mrs O'Leary explained. "At least Lord Russell is ashamed of

57

the English. He's too late to be sorry. They're the ones that drove us from our homes and put us on this ship to America."

"Nobody drove me on to the ship, Ma. I walked!"

The woman sighed and wrapped an arm around his thin shoulders. "Thirty years ago when I was a lass it was different. Ireland wasn't rich, but it wasn't so very poor either. I can still remember my da, that's your grand-da, coming back from the French Wars. We didn't know it was the start of our troubles!"

"Grand-da started the bad times?"

"No, no, no! It was all the soldiers coming back to Ireland together. There were no jobs for them and precious little food to feed them," Mr O'Leary explained.

"Where did all the food go?" Seamus asked.

"Into English mouths and English bellies," Mr O'Leary said bitterly. "They charged us so much tax that we had to send all our best corn and cattle over to England while we went hungry."

"Is that when we started eating people?" the boy asked.

His mother jabbed a bony finger at him. "Stop that, Seamus, I'm warning you."

The boy fell silent and sat on the swaying deck while men began to hurry towards the hatches with water pumps. Dirty green water was pumped over the side of the ship into the darkening air.

"Are we sinking, Da?"

"No, son. Every ship takes on a little water," the man said. "Old buckets like this take on a little more, that's all."

"And what did the people eat when the English took our corn and cattle if they didn't eat … I mean … what *did* they eat?" Seamus asked with a sudden switch of subject.

"Potatoes, son, potatoes!" his mother smiled and stroked his red hair. "They were the saving of Ireland. Potatoes were easy to grow, they filled us up, they kept over the winter and we could even feed them to the pigs, then eat the pigs. A wonderful thing the potato."

Seamus frowned as he struggled to remember what a potato tasted like.

"Give a hand!" someone called and Mr O'Leary rose and he crossed the deck to help with the pumping.

"So why are we going to America?"

"Because potatoes didn't pay the rents," his mother told him. "When the rent collectors called they wanted cash or corn or cattle. They didn't want our poor potatoes. A lot of people were thrown off their farms because they couldn't pay their rents."

"Where did they go?"

"On the roads. They wandered off to the cities to beg for food or to find a job. But a lot died by the roadside. They say Lord Lucan threw forty-thousand Irish farmers off his land because they couldn't pay their rent."

"Did he throw us out, Ma?"

"No. Your grandfather had a little pension from the French Wars and that kept us going. We could have scraped a living if it hadn't been for the blight."

"Is that when the potatoes went rotten?" Seamus asked.

"It is, son, it is. The potatoes looked fine, but when you cut them open they were black and had the stench of death about them. That winter they say three-quarters of Ireland's potatoes were diseased by the blight."

"Did the people go hungry?"

"They starved. They died in their thousands, Seamus. Some just shrivelled away in their homes – some took to the roads and died in the ditches. There were too many bodies and the people were too poor to afford coffins. They just wrapped their loved ones in straw and buried them in ditches. That's what we did with your grand-da. But at least your father was strong enough to bury him deep. Some of the weaker ones just covered their dead ones with stones. Of course the dogs got them and scattered their bones along the roads."

The boy shuddered and his mother tightened her grip on his sharp-boned shoulders. "And, before you ask, Seamus, that was the time when the stories started of folk eating the dead. But I never saw it in our village, Seamus, never. So don't you go believing that Michael Mulloy."

"What did we eat then, Ma?"

"You remember we ate nettle soup?"

"I liked that!" the boy said brightly.

"I had to fill it out with grass and roots but it was all we had. We couldn't go to the workhouses, they were full. But we survived, we survived."

"So why are we leaving now?"

"Because there's a dreadful disease in the country. It's called typhus. There's not a village you can walk through that you don't hear the church bells ring for the dead. Your da and I decided the only way to escape was to take ship for America. We sold your grand-da's old sword and uniform and fine boots from the French Wars. We scraped enough to buy the tickets. This ship was the cheapest, son, because it's old and slow."

"When will we get there?"

"A couple of weeks, God willing," Mrs O'Leary smiled.

"What are those men doing?" Seamus asked.

In the near darkness a lantern glowed at the stern of the ship. In its light a group of sailors were lowering a rowing boat. The passengers on the deck who'd been pumping stopped their work and wandered back to see what they were doing. "Are you leaving us, lads?" Mr O'Leary shouted. "Rats deserting a sinking ship, is it?"

The captain stepped into the boat and wrapped a hand around the rope that held it. "We've sprung a plank, gentlemen. We're not far from the Irish shore so we'll just row back and collect some tar and oakum. You'll be safe if you stay at anchor and keep pumping. We'll be back at first light. Don't worry!" he called.

The Irish passengers moved towards the crew at the rowing boat. The crew jumped nimbly into the boat as the captain released the rope and let them drop into the dark-green waters under the shadow of the ship's stern.

They disappeared as night fell over the heaving sea. The ship creaked. There was the steady sucking of water below the deck then the waves began to splash over the side rail. Mrs O'Leary jumped to her feet and clutched the match-thin child to herself.

The men at the pumps gave up when they saw it was hopeless. Without anyone giving an order the Irish moved towards one another and gathered in a circle on the main deck. They knelt. They lowered their heads and put their hands together.

"Our Father..." someone began praying and 80 voices joined in. As the water lapped over their knees a few tried to raise the children up to the rigging, out of the way of the foaming waters. Most simply rose to their feet and began singing a hymn. They were still singing when a larger wave turned the ship and tumbled them to a swirling green death that was merciful and quick.

There is no doubt that the British government and the English landowners could have done more to help the Irish peasants. When the Irish were short of food and money the British government offered the peasants work. They set up road-building schemes so the Irish could earn money to buy food and pay rent. But the work was back-breaking and badly paid – the starving and weak men, women and children built roads that led to nowhere. The work only helped to kill them quicker – some towns reported up to 150 deaths every day.

The British didn't even offer the Irish much sympathy for their miseries. One Prime Minister sneered that "The Irish are not capable of ruling themselves or surviving by themselves." The leading Victorian poet, Alfred Tennyson said spitefully:

"The Celts are all born furious fools. They live in a horrible island. Couldn't someone blow up that horrible island with dynamite and carry it off in pieces – a long way off?"

Over a million died of starvation or disease during the famine. A further million set sail for a new life in America, but that didn't solve their problems. Many of the vessels were too old and frail for the voyage and disappeared without trace; others were so filthy that most of the passengers died of disease before they arrived.

And there was no warm welcome from the Americans. The Irish were offered cellars to live in and jobs were advertised with signs saying "No Irish". Disease swept through the New York slums where the Irish crowded together. They died more miserably than if they had stayed in the green fields of home.

The Irish weren't the first, and they certainly won't be the last, to die of a famine.

Famine Disasters

1. Egypt. The famous seven-year famine starting in 1708 bc is described in the Bible where the hero is Joseph. But there was an earlier famine in 3500 bc that was one of the first disasters to be recorded in writing. An inscription on a tomb said:

I am mourning on my high throne for this great misfortune. The waters of the Nile have failed us for seven years and food is short. Each man has become a thief to his neighbour. The child cries, the youth creeps along, the heads of the old are bowed down. The food stores are torn open but instead of grain there is air. Everything is exhausted.

In AD 1064 famine returned to Egypt and this time brought with it the terrors of cannibalism. Hungry bands waited in upstairs rooms, lowered hooks on ropes and snatched up passing strangers to murder and eat.

In the next famine, AD 1200, children were caught, killed and roasted like lambs. Reports even said that parents ate their own children. A visiting doctor from Baghdad said he witnessed this himself. He reported, "I myself saw a small roasted child in a basket. They carried it in to the Emir (Prince) and brought in the child's mother and father. The Emir sentenced both of them to be burnt alive." Once the cannibals were roasted, the witnesses were allowed to eat them!

Friends were invited to a house and told, "We'd like you to

come for dinner!" Little did those friends suspect that they *were* the dinner. Even repairmen were called to houses and killed for food while they worked.

The AD 1200 famine in Egypt seems to have been one of the most savage eras in history.

2. **England, 1069.** Don't imagine cannibalism only happened outside Europe. When the Normans invaded England in 1066 they destroyed lands in the north from Durham to York. Northern people had tried to fight the Normans and burning their farms and killing their animals was meant to be a lesson to the rest of England. Some survived and a history of the time says...

Many were forced to eat dogs, cats, rats and other loathsome and vile vermin. Yea, and some did not hesitate to eat the flesh of men.

3. **China, 1867-68.** Egypt may have been the most horrific famine, but the most deadly was in China. Three years without a drop of rain killed over 10 million people and affected another 70 million in northern and central China. Travelling on the roads was suicide as bands of starving men murdered travellers and ate their camels, horses or donkeys from under them. The sights were horrific. A foreign visitor reported:

Night travel was out of the question. The road was littered by the skeletons of men and beasts. The wolves, dogs and foxes soon put an end to the sufferings of any wretch who lay down to recover from his sickness in those terrible valleys.

The government did not tell the rest of the world of the famine at the time so very little outside help got through.

F
A
C
T
O
F
I
L
E

Stories did get out of pits dug that were vast graves, each one big enough to take 10,000 bodies.

Parents were said to kill their children to end their suffering; they then killed themselves by drowning in wells or taking arsenic poison. Other parents sold their children as slaves then used the money to buy food – a little girl could be bought for two dollars and a married woman for six.

In 1942 the war with Japan, war within China and another drought brought famine and suffering back to Honam Province. People were left to eat the bark off trees while the dead were cooked and eaten.

4. **Africa, 198-88.** The Sahara Desert is creeping south as rainfall reduced by 25 per cent in the 1980s and 90s.

Africa is a poor continent at the best of times but the civil wars that have raged through some countries have brought famine and death for millions.

Ethiopia suffered drought, famine and civil war between 1984 and 1986. While the poor people starved, the government celebrated being in power for 10 years. They spent 200 million dollars on those celebrations as hundreds died every day! The rains arrived in 1986 but the problems remained. The United Nations sent in food supplies, only to see guerrilla fighters destroy the lorries and burn the food before it reached the hungry people.

Money was sent to Ethiopia – a million dollars a day. But the country was ruled by the army and they were the ones who got the food.

It isn't enough for the rich countries to send help to disaster regions. Someone has to make sure the help gets through to the people who need it.

5. Russia, 1921-23. In the past 1,000 years Russia has suffered 100 famines. When a drought struck in 1921 the problem was made worse by the new government, which was fighting rebels. A visitor from Britain described the scene:

In almost every home there were benches covered with birch or lime leaves. These are dried, beaten, mixed with acorns, some soil and water. This mixture is baked into something they call bread but which smells more like cooked manure. The government records show that nine out of every ten children aged one to three have already died from the famine.

Children were gathered into special homes to save them. In fact, the homes packed six to a bed and made it easy for deadly diseases to spread. The bodies were cleared out every day and put into a shed to wait for the collection cart that had a regular job going from home to home.

When the famine ended in 1923, one of the biggest problems was finding enough leather saddles and harnesses for the farm animals – the old ones had all been eaten by the starving peasants.

6. USA, 1909-14 and 1934-41. The USA is the world's richest country by far so it's hard to imagine people suffering a famine there. But in the early twentieth century farmers moved on to

the dried plains and hoped for rain. The old folk legend was that "the rain will follow the plough". In other words, "start digging in dry ground, plant some seeds and the rain will arrive". That's nonsense, of course and it didn't work: the farmers suffered a drought from 1909 to 1914.

But there are many people who are happy to cash in on other people's disasters. And "rain-makers" arrived in the West to charge the farmers for "making" rain. That didn't work either.

Some westerners believed that explosions shook the rain out of passing clouds. They set off dozens of dynamite explosions. That didn't work.

In the end nature brought the rain, but many farmers had been ruined by then.

The drought of 1934 was a little different. The farmers had planted crops and made a fortune during the years of the First World War (1914-18). They then tried to return the fields to grass for animals afterwards. But the ploughing had loosened the soil, the farmers failed to seed it with new grass, cattle hooves loosened it further and drought dried it up. The American Midwest ended as a vast "Dust Bowl". When strong winds came along, the farmers' soil was blown away. You can't farm on rock so the cattle starved and so did the farmers. Some cattle even suffocated when the dust blocked their nostrils.

Ten years of normal rainfall brought the grass back. But by then thousands of farmers had moved to the cities and died homesick and poor ... just as some of their Irish ancestors must have done almost 100 years before.

OUT OF THE SKY

Disasters can happen through the force of nature or human carelessness. But sometimes they are created quite deliberately. Someone decides that their fellow humans will die. It is a disaster for the innocent victims and their families, but in the eyes of the law it is worse ... it is mass murder.

The BAe 146 air disaster, California, November 1987

There was a tiny twitch in the right cheek of David Burke. You would think he was a handsome young man, normal and calm ... except for that tiny twitch. David Burke's blue uniform jacket and white shirt were spotless and uncreased. He looked perfect ... except for the twitch. It showed most when he smiled and he was trying to smile now.

He sat across the desk from an older man in glasses with thick, brown rims and listened carefully. "What's the problem, Ray?" Burke asked cheerfully.

The sign on the man's desk said, "Ray Martin – Personnel Manager, Pacific Southwest Airlines". Martin pushed a bundle of papers across the desk. "These are some of your accounts for the last month."

"They are!" Burke agreed cheerfully.

"You see this bill?" the man in glasses asked, tapping the top paper. "It's for a round of drinks you served on a flight on 7 November. It says $23. But those drinks cost $25."

Burke shrugged. "An easy mistake to make."

Martin shook his head slowly. "It's not a mistake. The drinks cost twenty five dollars and you charged the passenger twenty five dollars. If you look really closely you'll see this bill has been altered from twenty-five to twenty-three. The airline received twenty-three. What happened to the other two dollars?"

Burke's cheek twitched furiously. He rubbed it with his right hand to disguise it. "You tell me, Ray!"

Martin leaned forward. "It went into your pocket, Burke. You robbed the airline."

"Hey! Robbed! Two lousy dollars! Robbed is a bit of a strong word, Ray."

"No, Burke. Not *two* dollars. Sixty-nine this month. I'm sure if we checked back over the year we'd find a lot more. Pacific Southwest does not tolerate thieves. You are fired."

Burke's easy smile faded. "I was planning on getting married in a couple of months' time. I need this job, Ray."

"You should have thought of that before you defrauded the company."

Burke clenched his fists. "How do I explain this to my parents?"

"You should have thought of that before cheating us."

"The shame of it ... they were so proud of me when I got the job..."

"They have a right to know they raised a liar for a son," Martin went on coldly.

"Give me a break. Have a little pity, Ray! One more chance. For the sake of my parents. For Louise. We're getting married. It won't happen again, Ray, I swear it."

Ray Martin pushed the heavy spectacles back on to his nose and looked down at some letters on his desk. "No," he said. "Get out. Collect your last wage packet from the desk, hand in your uniform tomorrow and then don't come back."

"I'll need a reference from you to get another job."

"No chance."

David Burke rose slowly to his feet, the right side of his face stiff and frozen in a grin. The left side of his face showed no expression. "I owe you one, Ray," he said as he backed towards the door.

"You owe Pacific Southwest sixty-nine dollars, to be exact," Martin said cruelly. "You will find it has been deducted from your final pay packet. Now get out."

David Burke collected his pay and left the airline building. His right cheek was still now and his walk was determined. He walked a block and stopped at a shop window. He fingered the cash in his pocket and walked into the shop.

"You have a gun in the window ... a .44 Magnum."

"Yes, sir."

"I'd like to buy it. With a box of ammunition."

"You'll need to get a police permit. What's it for?" the old man behind the counter asked.

"Vermin," Burke said.

"You want a shotgun for rats, son."

"Nah! Only joking. I need a pistol for self-defence," Burke said, the easy smile returning. "Something to keep in my bedside drawer."

"Very wise," the old man nodded, taking a box from under the counter and passing it across to his customer. "There are a lot of lunatics around that would rob you for the gold fillings in your teeth! That'll be sixty-nine dollars, sir."

"That'll be right," Burke said, handing over the cash. "It's amazing what sixty-nine dollars will get you."

"It gets you firepower," the old man said.

"It gets you fired," Burke said grimly.

"What's that?"

"A private joke," the young man murmured.

"Take the gun now, show me proof of your address and you register it with the police as soon as possible."

"Will do," Burke nodded and walked out of the shop with the box under his arm.

David Burke had a lot to do and worked quickly that day. When he reached his flat he phoned the airline. "Hi, Jane!" he said cheerfully. "Is Ray Martin booked on the usual flight tomorrow morning? Flight twenty-oh-nine? He is? Look ... could you book me a staff ticket on the same flight? We have a meeting and it would save time if we could meet on the plane. Great! Thanks Jane. I owe you one."

The rest of that evening he spent studying the pistol and the instructions. He couldn't fire it in his flat but he seemed happy that he could handle it when he needed to.

David Burke slept badly – the twitch in his cheek was painful now.

He rose early and showered and dressed in his airline uniform, the trousers perfectly creased. His watch showed it was 9:15

when he picked up the phone. He dialled the number and waited for the answerphone to finish speaking. "Hi, Louise. Sorry I missed you. Probably best that we don't talk. This is just to say goodbye." He paused a long while then went on. "I was trying to raise the money we needed to get married. I guess I tried too hard. Now I've no job and no future. Ray Martin has seen to that. It's just not fair, Louise. So I'm going to even up the score. Don't cry for me. I'm a loser – you'll be better off without me. Love you, Lou. Goodbye."

He put the phone down gently, took a briefcase from his bed and put the pistol inside it. He slipped on his spotless blue jacket and left the flat, locking the door carefully.

Burke took the usual bus to the airport and arrived in time for the 9:30 flight. He crossed the crowded lounge to the Pacific Southwest desk. "Hi, Jane, got my ticket?"

"Right next to Mr Martin," the young black woman said.

"Say, could you change that for the seat behind him?" Burke asked.

"But I thought you wanted to meet with him," Jane frowned.

"I have work I need to do. Don't want to be stuck with old Ray Martin the whole journey!" he laughed.

She raised a knowing eyebrow and handed him the altered ticket. Looking across the lounge she said, "There he goes now. Over there."

The left side of Burke's face stiffened and the right side began to twitch. He didn't seem keen to join his ex-manager. "Have you heard I'm leaving Pacific Southwest?" he asked.

The woman nodded. "Someone said. Got another job to go to?"

"I guess you could say I'm going to a better place," David Burke answered and the right side of his face smiled. He looked through the lounge windows and across the tarmac to where his BAe 146 commuter jet waited. Then he looked at the hazy blue winter sky beyond it.

"Have a nice day," Jane told him.

"I will, thank you, Jane. I will."

He turned and walked towards the departure corridor where passengers were walking through the barrier. There was a sharp buzz and a security guard stopped an elderly woman. "Check your bag, ma'am?" he asked. "Metal detector says you have something metal inside there."

It turned out to be a bunch of keys and the woman was allowed to pass through. Burke stood beside the guard. "Busy day, George?"

"Every day's a busy day, Mr Burke."

David Burke opened the small gate next to the guard and stepped through as staff usually did. "Kids all right, George?"

"Wild as ever, Mr Burke," the guard laughed and turned back to the barrier which was buzzing again.

David Burke slapped him on the back. "Have a nice day, George," he said.

Burke crossed the tarmac, boarded the plane and prepared to complete his plan of revenge. He timed it so that he was one of the last passengers to arrive and slipped into his seat behind Ray Martin.

The plane climbed out of the city haze and into the brilliant blue.

It took the crash investigators a little while to piece together what happened next.

An air-sickness bag was found in the wreckage. A message was written on it by David Burke. It read:

Hi, Ray,
I think it's sort of strange that we end up like this. I asked for pity for the sake of my family, remember? Well, I got none and you'll get none.
David

Burke must have passed the bag to his former boss – a tap on the shoulder, a startled jump from Martin seeing the man he'd fired the day before. Seeing him still in the PSA blue uniform.

That letter a little touch to add to Martin's terror before Burke took the gun from the case and shot him.

The crew would have heard the shot and the terrified screams of the helpless passengers. They were trapped on a plane with a murderer and there was no way out. They could pray and hope he'd finished his killing; hope that his revenge was complete with the death of Martin.

But David Burke had only just begun.

The first sign back on the ground that there was a problem was an urgent call from the pilot. "Hello control! There has been a gunshot in the passenger compartment ... a passenger has been shot ... a man in an airline steward's uniform has shot a passenger ... the victim is an employee of PSA ... we have a problem."

Then, over the radio came a second voice. "And I'm the problem!"

This was followed by two explosions as the pilot and co-pilot were shot.

The other 40 innocent people died along with David Burke when the aircraft plunged to the ground.

Like many other disasters, the lessons of the BAe 146 disaster in California were learned too late. And they weren't acted on thoroughly enough.

The investigation board were horrified to discover how easy it was to smuggle a weapon on to an aircraft. Passengers passed through a metal detector and their identity was checked before they were allowed on to a plane. But people like David Burke who worked for the airline were waved through. They could be carrying anything.

After Burke's revenge attack the airline workers were checked just the same as other passengers. That still failed to prevent an air disaster a year later. Workers were still allowed on to the runway to check planes and load them with baggage. Pan Am flight 103 left Heathrow for New York three days before Christmas 1988. It had been loaded with baggage while it stood at Heathrow and it seems certain that one of the loaders placed a bomb in the luggage compartment. It exploded at 9,500 metres over the small town of Lockerbie in Scotland. Not only did all 249 passengers and crew die, but 11 residents of the town were killed by falling wreckage.

The Lockerbie priest spoke for many when he said, "What can you do but weep?"

Only after this disaster were all staff checked when entering the security area around aircraft.

Air Disasters

Flying is still one of the safest forms of transport. If a baby was born on a flying jumbo jet and never got off it then it would be around 82 years before it met with an accident! Or to put it another way, an accident happens once every 430 million minutes of flying time.

The problem is that when aircraft crash there is a poor chance of surviving. There are many ways in which aircraft can be involved in a disaster. A few of the most spectacular include...

1. Shot down. War planes risk being shot down by fire from the ground or other aircraft. It's rare for passenger planes to be shot down. But that's what happened in 1983 to a Korean Airlines 747 jet. It strayed off its planned flight path and flew over secret missile test sites in the Soviet Union. Soviet fighter planes destroyed the 747, killing all 269 aboard. The Soviet government said it was a spy plane and ignored warnings to change course. Within a year they changed their story and admitted it was a mistake. It's still a mystery as to why the plane was 300 miles off course – had the pilots' navigation computer gone wrong? Or were they, as some experts have suggested, taking a short cut to save fuel and cut costs? We'll probably never know.

2. Fire. Aircraft are heavier than air so if they lose power the pilot cannot always make a safe landing. But carrying passengers under a floating bag of gas was considered much safer. Airships were built that could travel thousands of miles without fear of crashing. The German airship *Hindenburg* was the largest airship ever built at almost 300 metres long, and in the year it was built, 1936, it covered 186,000 safe miles. On 3 May 1937 it came in to land in New Jersey after crossing the Atlantic. An electrical spark probably started the fire that caught the inflammable hydrogen in the gas bag and the airship sank to the ground as a ball of fire. Amazingly only 36 of the 97 people aboard died. An American radio commentator was making a live broadcast of the landing and his horrified report has never been forgotten. "This is the worst thing I've ever witnessed!" he sobbed.

3. **Ice.** On 13 January 1982 an Air Florida passenger jet attempted to take off in a blizzard. Slush on the Washington runway slowed it, and ice on the wings meant it struggled to rise over a railway bridge across the Potomac River. As it reached a road bridge, a wheel caught the highway and the plane dived into the Potomac, sweeping several cars with it. The fuselage broke open and icy water rushed in before passengers could unbuckle their seatbelts. Incredibly, a subway train with 1,000 passengers crashed in Washington just a few minutes after the Air Florida jet. Emergency services were stretched beyond their limits. Helicopters swarmed over the scene of the crash – some to rescue and some to film the disaster for ghoulish television audiences. Among the heroes was a passenger who was in reach of a helicopter rescue rope and five times passed it to other passengers in greater need than himself. When the helicopter returned a sixth time he had vanished under the ice. A rescue worker said: "I've never seen such guts. It seemed to me he decided that the women and injured men needed to get out of there before him and even as he was going under he stuck to that decision."

4. **Collision.** The worst nightmare of any pilot is to collide with another plane. It is a rare thing to happen. But in March 1977 two jumbo jets collided at the airport in Tenerife in the Atlantic – both planes were full of holidaymakers. On a foggy day one of the jets tried to take off on a runway while the other jet was taxiing across. When the pilot of the rising plane saw the other he tried to lift into the air and "hop" over the obstruction but his tail caught the second plane and he came down on top of it. Only 61 people survived; 583 died, making it the worst disaster in flying history.

5. **Pilot error.** Many air crashes are blamed on the pilots, even when they have been killed and can't defend themselves. In 1989 a Brazilian pilot became a hero when he brought his lost passenger jet down in the Amazon jungle with the loss of "only" 13 lives. Reporters thought at first the hero pilot had suffered because his navigation computer had failed. Investigators found that he had set up the computer wrongly because he had been too busy listening to a Brazil-Chile football match on the radio. But some mistakes are harder to understand. An RAF pilot took off everything that felt uncomfortable when he was flying – the aircraft began to fail so he jumped out ... and forgot that he'd taken off his "uncomfortable" parachute!

6. **Aircraft failure.** The first fatal air crash happened to the inventor of the aeroplane, Orville Wright, when a propeller broke and the plane fell to the ground. Orville survived but his passenger, Thomas Selfridge, died. Ninety years later air crashes still happen through no fault of the pilot but because of a fault in the aircraft. The more complicated modern planes become the more there is to go wrong! In 1972 a DC10 aircraft lost a door through a faulty lock. This caused the fuselage to buckle and the controls to fail. Only brilliant piloting brought the American Airlines plane safely in to land at Ontario. The door locks were checked and replacement locks were designed. But for some reason some DC10s were allowed to leave the factory without them. So two years later in 1974 another DC10 lost its door; this time, the 12 crew and 334 passengers were killed when the Turkish Airlines plane crashed in Ermonville Forest near Paris.

7. Fog. If you are in a lift in one of the world's tallest buildings you may worry about an accident ... but you would not expect to be the victim of an air accident. Yet that's what happened to Betty Lou Oliver in 1945. A US Air Force bomber became lost in the fog and smashed into the side of the Empire State Building, making a six-metre hole in the 78th floor. One of the engines shot across the floor, smashed into the lift shaft and plunged down. Betty Lou was a lift operator and the crashing engine snapped the cable on her lift. She dropped from the 76th floor to the basement. She survived, though her back and legs were broken. A passing doctor helped her out then he ran up 79 flights of stairs and carried an injured woman down. The fire service had the flames extinguished in just 40 minutes. Only 14 people died, while 1,500 were rescued.

8. Lightning. In 1975 a passenger jet came in to land at New York's Kennedy Airport but struck the landing lights and crashed on to a motorway. Amazingly, no cars were hit and even though the plane burst into flames there were 14

F A C T O F I L E

survivors from the 116 passengers on board. Witnesses swore that the plane had been struck by lightning, but experts said this was not the cause. "Lightning strikes on aircraft are common but seldom result in damage," one expert said. "Only the really severe ones are ever reported." The flashes the witnesses saw were probably caused by the plane scything through electric cables. Investigators blamed a sudden freak wind, but there is still a suspicion that a bolt of lightning hit the plane.

INTO THE SEA

Disasters sometimes make heroes of people who always thought they were normal and unheroic. What makes a hero? Maybe it's someone who fights on when most of us would give up. Maybe it's someone who thinks of others and puts their safety first...

The *Estonia* ferry disaster, Baltic Sea, September 1994

A hero? No, I don't think I'm a hero. On that dreadful night I did what I had to do. I didn't *think* about it. Looking back, and thinking about it *now*, I tremble. In my nightmares I feel the unbelievable cold and I see again the face of the girl. I wake up and I'm going through it all again.

My name is Henrik. I'm a student and I live in Stockholm, Sweden. I've no relatives – just a few good friends who'd cry for me if I died. What else do you need to know about me?

Only about my experiences that night at the end of September. On the ferry from Estonia back to Sweden.

Why did I decide to go to Estonia?

Shopping! Lots of people do it. It's a few hours' trip across the Baltic Sea and everything is so cheap in the shops that it's worth the ferry fare. Then it's the adventure, isn't it? There's something crazy about crossing a sea to shop in a foreign country, don't you think?

At least, that's what I *used* to think. Never again!

Estonia is a poor country. That's why everything in the shops is so cheap. Everything *modern* in Estonia is the pride of the country. Even their car ferry. It carried cars, lorries and passengers across the Baltic Sea into Scandinavia. It was painted in blue and white – the country's national flag colours – and of course they had to name it after the country – the *Estonia*.

I enjoyed wandering round the old capital city of Tallinn for too long. Shopping, and trying to find a good camera cheap. Then I looked at my watch – a cheap Russian one – and saw how late it was getting. I raced to the bus station and caught the last bus to the ferry.

I reached the terminal around 6:30. "A cabin for Stockholm, please," I panted as I ran into the booking office.

The assistant was a sneering old man who seemed to take great pleasure in telling me, "You should have booked earlier if you wanted a cabin. Only one cabin left. There's a late booking charge of twenty krona," he added with a cruel grin.

There was no point in counting the money in my pocket. It was no more than five krona. Instead I gave him my friendliest smile. "Then I'll just take a deck ticket, please."

He looked out of the front window of the office where the wind was growing stronger every minute. "You are in for a sleepless night," he said.

Maybe the man was a prophet. He didn't know how true those last words were.

I climbed the swaying gangway on to the ferry. The front of the ship was open ... the whole of the bows lifted up on a hinge. The last cars were being guided into this hungry mouth as I found my way to the shelter of the restaurant.

I dropped my bags by a table. The driving rain had soaked my coat and I shook the dampness out of it before I walked to the counter and sorted my money. A hot meal would have taken my last krona. I ordered a sandwich. If I'd known it could have been my *last* meal I'd have spent that last krona. After all, money's no use when you're lying on the bottom of the ocean.

But I bought a sandwich because I thought we'd arrive safely in Stockholm the next morning. I really believed that. I know some people said they felt that something was going to happen. Some sixth sense warned them that danger was ahead. I can honestly say that I had no fear whatsoever.

They weren't a very lively bunch of people that night. A group of about 50 pensioners from just south of Stockholm were talking quietly in the restaurant. I remember them now, because they were the ones who had least chance of survival.

And I remember a father and son. I don't know much Estonian, but the language is a little like Swedish. The boy was crying. "My teddy bear. I want my teddy bear."

"We'll go to the cabin and I'll tuck you up for the night," the man said.

"Can't sleep without my teddy," the little boy wailed.

"You are very tired," the man said. "You'll sleep."

"Teddy won't," the boy sniffed.

The man gave a broad grin. "Don't worry about that!" he said. "Mummy will look after it for you! Now let's go down to the cabin."

He led the boy to the stairs down to the sleeping-berths. That was the last I saw of them.

It was probably my sixth journey across the Baltic Sea, but this was the roughest. The ferry was pitching up and down and rolling from side to side. A group of young people carrying drinks staggered as if they were drunk. There was a lot of laughter as they spilled half their drinks on the rolling floor.

The restaurant was becoming stuffy so I decided to take a walk around the deck and catch a breath of fresh air. The sleet and spray was driving so hard that it struck me in the face with a stinging force. Ten seconds was all the fresh air I could take.

A dance band set up in the room next to the restaurant and couples drifted in to dance. I wanted to keep an eye on my shopping and I was tired after a day of walking the cold streets of Tallinn. I stayed where I was.

The warmth wrapped itself around me and I closed my eyes. It must have been just after ten o'clock when I fell into a deep sleep.

What woke me up was the *silence*. The disco band had stopped playing in the room next door – but there was something else that bothered me. People drifted away from the dance area disappointed and swayed into the restaurant. Tables began to slide across the floor. Cups and saucers shattered.

"What's wrong?" I asked a couple of dancers. "The band can't play while the ship is rolling like this," a young man said.

Then I realized what was *really* bothering me. The ship wasn't humming with the sound of its engines. I'd done some sailing back home in Sweden and I knew what that meant. A powerless boat will turn sideways on to the wind. Then it will begin to roll. If it's top heavy then it will roll over completely.

I tried to rise but a wave caught the ship and turned it almost on its side. It threw me to my knees. I struggled to my feet and was almost crushed as a huge drinks machine crashed to the floor.

That was a big wave. Somewhere someone screamed. Crew members began to hurry through the rooms calling, "Can you all go on deck, please, we have a small problem."

The small problem was that the ship didn't recover from that last roll. Cars and lorries on the vehicle decks broke loose and crashed against the side of the ship. It stayed tilted to that side. The door from the restaurant to the deck was just five metres away, but my feet slipped on the polished wooden floor. It was like climbing a glacier. My hands tried to claw at the smooth surface.

I know it sounds stupid, but it took me a while to realize I was still clinging on to my precious shopping bags. It was one of the hardest things I've ever done to let them go and watch them slide down the floor.

Now I was able to climb on all fours. Still it took me two minutes to cover those five metres.

How would the people in the cabins manage, I wondered. They had to climb from below decks while the ship lay at this crazy angle. Those old people. They'd never make it. I thanked the nasty little ticket clerk in Tallinn who had tried to overcharge me for a cabin. He'd given me a chance to survive.

I was sure that the ship was sinking. I tugged at the door to the restaurant, turned the handle and the door was smashed inwards by the force of the gale. The first wave that hit me soaked me to the skin. It was so cold I could scarcely breathe.

I clung to the rail of the ship and made my way towards the groups of people struggling to free the life rafts. Of course, a life raft is designed to be dropped into the sea. The angle of the ship was so steep they were being lowered on to the side, where they slid down. When they hit the sea it was a matter of luck whether they landed the right way up.

I watched one slide down the side and saw it land the right way up.

It was now or never. I slid down the side and hit the water a second or two after it. My speed was so great that I went deep below the surface. I struggled to tear my way back to the air. Stinging salt water forced its way into my nostrils, my boots felt like lead diver's boots and zigzags of light began to dance in front of my eyes.

I finally felt my head break the surface, I snatched at the precious air and let the next wave lift me. It not only lifted me, it smashed me against the side of the sinking ship.

As a ship sinks it sucks everything on the surface down with it. I knew I had to swim away from it as quickly as I could. Above me the sky cleared and the moon came out from behind its cloud cover. The scene became clear for a minute. I saw a life raft and headed towards it. Getting to the side of the raft wasn't such a problem. Climbing into it was.

A thin girl with fair hair plastered to the side of her head reached out a hand and tugged at me. The weight of my waterlogged clothes kept me in the water. A few moments later I felt a push from behind. A young man in the water was heaving me into the raft. As I flopped on to the floor I hadn't time to stop and catch my breath. I knew I had to return the favour. I turned and dragged him in after me. Over his shoulder I could see the ferry disappearing below the water in a smoking haze of red. Five minutes. That's all it took to sink.

He had the uniform of a crew member and the strong grip of a seaman as he shook hands. "I'm Mats."

"Henrik."

"Anyone else out there?" he asked.

"I can't see anyone," I told him.

"You're lucky," he said. He was an Estonian. "To swim through this sea with no lifejacket!"

"Life jacket?" I said. No one had been handing out life jackets on the *Estonia* but I'd remembered people snatching them before they went into the rafts. "No time," I said. What I really meant was that I had been too panicked.

The girl was huddled in a corner, shivering like a half-drowned cat. That's when I realized how cold I was. Getting out of the water hadn't saved my life. It had only delayed my death by a few hours. Instead of a nice quick drowning I was going to freeze slowly and painfully.

There was only one source of warmth for the three of us on the boat – human warmth. I slid across to the girl and put an arm around her. "I'm Henrik," I said. She looked at me blankly. The sailor joined us and we huddled together.

He spoke to the girl and she nodded stiffly. He looked across at me. "She's from Tartu. Her language is more like Hungarian."

I tried again. "Me, Henrik!"

She was too shocked to reply. Slowly her eyes began to close and I knew that this was how death took you. Give up hope and your life has nothing to cling on to. I became angry. More angry than I'd ever been in my life. I was in a rage at the unfairness of it all. I shook the girl and spoke to her until she was forced to listen.

I said the craziest things. "We'll be rescued soon ... we'll be in Sweden in the morning ... once we've warmed up and dried out we'll go out together. We'll have a few drinks in the Viking Bar in Stockholm, right? You, me and Mats. Isn't that right, Mats?"

Mats translated for me. The girl looked up at me as if I was crazy. Maybe I *was*. She smiled shyly and began to talk.

In the next four hours we were hit by everything the sea could throw at us. Blasts of hail, huge waves, then cruel and sudden calms that raised our hopes. We could hear the helicopters but they couldn't see us in the indigo darkness.

Still we talked to forget the cold. At last we began to slow down. Cold was draining the last of our energy. Then the girl looked up and pointed. The first sign of pearl grey light was staining the snow clouds. It was the encouragement we needed.

I think I had heard the life story of the girl and Mats; they had heard mine. I was even beginning to understand her language. As the helicopter's loop lowered into the life raft Mats and I agreed, "The girl first."

"You next," I told him. He was looking grey with the cold and I desperately wanted him to live. He shook my hand. That grip wasn't as strong as it had been five hours before.

Finally it was my turn to be winched up. At last I was able to let myself go. As I touched the floor of the helicopter I blacked out. I woke in hospital.

"Mats? The girl?" were my first questions.

"Safe," the doctor said. "You were the worst. Your body temperature was the lowest – just 30.5 degrees centigrade. You're lucky. And I understand you saved the girl."

I shook my head. I remembered the struggle to keep her awake. That's the secret of survival. It's not enough to *fight* – you have to fight *for* something … or some*one*. I fought for her. Look at it that way and you'll see that the truth is that *she* saved *my* life.

And did we ever get that drink in the Viking Bar? We did. But it wasn't a celebration. It was in memory of the others who weren't so lucky.

I've been to Hell, and it isn't burning red coals – it's icy indigo water.

The bow doors of the Estonia *were checked just before the ship sailed. The inspectors said the seals to keep out the water were weak … but they allowed the ferry to sail. The force of the driving gale weakened the outside door and water poured in. A crew member said video cameras showed the water rushing into the car decks. The ship's pumps were switched on but couldn't cope with that amount of water. When the water reached the engines they cut out and the fate of the ferry was decided. Only 138 of the 1,049 people on board the ferry were rescued.*

Sea Disasters

1. *Herald of Free Enterprise*, **1987.** In 1987 the ferry Herald of Free Enterprise sank off the coast of Holland when water entered a loading door. Fewer people died than on the *Estonia* because the weather conditions were not so fierce and the ship was nearer to port. The sea was not so cold either. The Baltic was 12ºC when the *Estonia* sank. A fit person could last no more than two hours in water of that temperature. Henrik's temperature of 30.5ºC was the lowest in his raft. But others were an incredible 26ºC when they were rescued (a person's normal temperature should be around 37ºC).

2. *Diana II*, **1993.** Following the *Herald of Free Enterprise* disaster, European ferries were made a lot safer. Ferry companies in Europe signed an agreement on new standards of safety. The owners of the *Estonia* had not signed this agreement because Estonia was not in the European Community. The *Estonia*'s sister ship, the *Diana II*, almost lost her bow doors just a year before the *Estonia* sank. The *Mariella* almost capsized when water came through the bow doors eight years earlier. No lessons were learned from these near misses.

3. The hero. One of the greatest acts of courage was seen during the *Herald of Free Enterprise* disaster. A Londoner, Andrew Parker, saw that there was a six-foot gap between the sinking ship and safety. He leaned across and made himself

F A C T O F I L E

into a human bridge. He remained there until 120 people had walked across him and only then did he allow himself to be rescued. He was awarded the George medal for bravery but the horror of the experience was a terrible price for him to pay.

4. *Kiangya*, **1948.** One of the most gruesome tales of a sinking comes from China in 1948. The Chinese steamer *Kiangya* began to sink with almost 3,000 aboard. Many of the old people feared death by drowning so they begged a ship's officer to take his pistol and shoot them. He agreed and carried out the killings before the ship sank.

5. *Titanic*, **1912.** The most famous disaster was probably the sinking of the *Titanic* in 1912. 1,403 people died when the "unsinkable" liner struck an iceberg in the Atlantic. As she left harbour her huge size "sucked" two smaller ships towards her. They almost collided. If they *had* crashed into the *Titanic* then the liner would have had to stop its voyage for repairs. She would never have then struck that iceberg. In escaping a small accident the *Titanic* went on to a much greater disaster.

6. *Morro Castle*, **1934.** On the *Titanic* many of the passengers and crew behaved with dignity and courage, giving up their place in the lifeboats to someone else. But a fire on the cruise ship *Morro Castle* in 1934 showed the nastier side of human nature. The captain had stomach pains and died – there was a rumour that he was poisoned. When the chief officer took command he was faced with the problem of a small fire in the passenger library. No one was worried because the owners said the *Morro Castle* was fireproof! The ship continued to speed over the North Atlantic towards New York and, of course, the speed whipped the flames through the decks. It was 3 a.m.

and most passengers were asleep – but no alarm was sounded to warn them. Some staggered on to the deck and jumped overboard without waiting for the lifeboats. One hundred and thirty-four of the 549 people aboard died. The ship drifted on to the shore and sightseers bought tickets to go and see what was the death spot of all those people.

7. *Exxon Valdez*, **1989**. Not all disasters cost human lives. When the oil tanker *Exxon Valdez* ran on to rocks in 1989 her crew were safe. But the oil that gushed out of her damaged hull killed thousands of fish along with 86,000 birds that fed on them, 1,000 otters and 200 seals. The oil slick covered 900 square miles and the attempts to clean it up were bungled – the oil companies and government were simply not prepared for such a vast spillage. They had struggled to clean up a spill of 1,500 barrels just three months before – the *Exxon Valdez* lost almost a quarter of a million barrels.

ALONGSIDE
MISTER DEATH

Human carelessness and stupidity can kill many. But it always seems that Nature can kill more. One of the greatest disasters of all time was the Black Death – a plague that swept across the world in the middle of the 1300s and returned time and again to claim more lives. The people of that time had no idea what caused the disease but they desperately wanted to believe that doctors could cure it.

The Black Death disaster, Italy, 1348

The little girl felt in the pocket of her dress and stroked the creature that nestled in its dark depths. "Oh, mousie, mousie! You're poorly, aren't you?"

She felt the creature tremble against her palm then pulled her hand out of her pocket as the door swung open. Her stern-faced nanny looked down at her. "How are we this morning, Miss Lucia?" she asked.

The girl tucked her fine dark hair behind her ears and whispered, "Better, Nurse Del Arte."

"We'll let the doctor look at you anyway. He's here now," the woman said. "He's come all the way from Florence and we don't want to waste his time, do we?"

"No, Nurse Del Arte."

When the man entered the room Lucia's heart jumped and she cowered back into her pillows. His head was covered by a hood and his face masked by a black scarf. Only his dark, fierce eyes could be seen.

But his voice, when he spoke, was soft and smooth as new butter. "Now, young lady, you have frightened your mother with your sickness. But you don't look too ill to me."

"No, Doctor," Lucia said and her voice was a croak. "Why are you wearing that mask?"

"The disease is spread on bad air, you know. I breathe through this silk and it helps me stay alive." He pulled a bunch of violets from the bag he was carrying and held them under his nose. He breathed deeply. "The scent of the flowers protects me too," he said. "Have flowers brought into the room," the doctor ordered.

Nurse Del Arte nodded slowly but didn't move.

"Have many people died?" Lucia asked, forgetting her fear.

He rested his cold, hard hand against her forehead. "You are warm, and that is not a good sign. Those with the plague burn with the fires of Hell," he murmured. "Children seem to suffer most. I've seen fifty dead within the week."

"Hush! You'll scare the child to death," Nurse Del Arte snapped.

The doctor shrugged. "Death comes to us all," he said. "It is better that she is prepared for it. Hold your foolish tongue, woman."

Lucia was shocked. No one spoke to Nurse Del Arte like that. But the woman's mouth shut like a rat-trap. "First you feel poorly," the doctor went on. "And then your body starts to swell. Lift your arms above your head." He reached under her armpits and pinched the skin. Lucia gasped. "No swelling there – not yet. Those who suffer the plague get large swellings under their armpits. These turn a deep violet, then black and begin to bleed. Then it's time for a visit from Old Mister Death!" the doctor said cheerfully.

"Mister Death!" Lucia said.

"We all meet him sooner or later. He is skeleton thin and bone white and dressed in a cloak of darkness. He carries a scythe with him but it's not for cutting corn. One touch of that scythe and you must follow him to the Land of Death!"

"Doctor!" the nurse cried. "There is no need to frighten the child so! She has no swelling under the arms. She's in no danger!"

The doctor shrugged. "Sometimes the victims get the swellings at the top of the legs. Of course, it would be wrong for me to examine a young lady in that way. But you could, Nurse."

The nanny stepped across to the bed and patted Lucia on the knee. "It's just a chill you have," she whispered. Then she slid her hand over the girl's dress till it rested at the top of her thigh. Her hand froze as it felt the soft swelling. She squeezed it. Lucia cried out. "Sorry, child, sorry!"

Lucia bit a knuckle. She knew the nanny had squeezed the life out of her friend Mousie.

"What have you found?" the doctor demanded.

"A soft lump," the nanny moaned.

The doctor rubbed his hands as soft as deerskin. "It's not too late!" he cried. "The child hasn't started spitting blood. There is no rash around her wrist. I think she can be saved!" He stopped and spread his soft, white hands. "But the medicines are rare and precious, you understand, Nurse? The young lady's parents are rich, are they not?"

"They own houses and lands from here to the Florence border," she replied proudly.

"And they have cash? Gold? Silver?"

Lucia put in, "Father has just returned from a raid on Florence. He took all the silver his horses could carry! He returned with bales of their finest silks and cloth of gold and..." The girl stopped. She remembered that she'd been looking at one bale of rich cloth when her little pet creature had crawled out and twitched its black whiskers at her and stared at her with fearless bright eyes. She slid a hand into her pocket. It was dead now.

The nanny gave a grim smile. "The people of Florence were so sick with the plague they couldn't stop your father. We've waited years for this revenge!"

The doctor was impatient. "So fetch the gold and I can start the cure."

The nanny turned to leave. The doctor hummed happily as he opened his deep bag and took out a bottle of dark blue glass. He dipped a silver spoon in and scooped up some fine green crystals. "This will purify your blood," he said.

"What is it?"

"These are emeralds from the Indies, crushed into a powder. The world's most precious jewels because they are the rarest!"

He was still holding the spoon up to the light when the nanny returned with a leather pouch. The doctor's eyes were fixed on the pouch. "Here's Nurse with a purse," he chuckled. "I was telling our young patient that these are powdered emeralds. One spoonful will cost a gold piece."

The nanny reached in and took one out. The doctor grasped it, pushed it under his silk mask and tested it with his teeth before slipping it into the pocket of his gown. He thrust the spoon at Lucia, she closed her eyes, took it in her mouth and swallowed the bitter crystals.

The doctor opened his bag again and took out a small leather bottle. He pulled out the stopper and dipped some of the liquid on to the tip of one finger. Then he rubbed the liquid into Lucia's forehead. She wrinkled her nose in disgust at the butcher-shop smell. "What's that?"

"The blood of puppy dog," the doctor said briskly. Lucia screwed up her face while the doctor replaced the stopper and held it out to the nanny. "Rub this in every hour."

When Nurse Del Arte reached out the doctor held back. "That will be another gold piece, if you please."

"It's a rich puppy dog you have there," the woman said sourly.

"A rare and special breed," the doctor shrugged, his eyes fixed on the purse that still had gold inside it.

"What else should I do?" the nanny asked.

"We must see that no one enters or leaves the house till the child recovers," the man said.

"Are *you* staying, then?" Nurse Del Arte asked.

The man waved his bunch of violet flowers. "I am safe from infection so I can leave to work my humble medicine among the needy," he said.

Lucia slipped a hand into her pocket and felt the dead animal. If she couldn't leave the house then she couldn't bury it in the churchyard. It wasn't fair that poor Mousie should be sealed in the sick-house with them. She took him out gently. The doctor was turned towards the nanny. Lucia slipped the little black corpse into his pocket that hung open with the weight of the gold.

"I have here some special onions," the doctor was saying. "One gold piece each."

The nanny's mouth fell open. "How many will we need?"

"How many gold pieces do you have," the doctor asked.

"Four left."

"Then have four onions. Slice them open and lay them on the floor of the room. The infected air will be sucked into the onions. Take them up and bury them deep."

"How long?" Lucia asked.

"Ten days," the doctor said. "Ten days, that's all. If Mister Death and his scythe haven't touched you by then you will live," he said snatching the purse and dropping it into his open pocket. He rose to his feet. "I will tell the sheriff that this house may be infected. He will send the corpse collectors round to paint a red cross on the door. But don't worry," he added, hurrying from the room, clutching violets to his nose. "If anyone else falls sick then call me. I am always here for the sick … so long as they have gold in their purses!"

And he was gone.

Lucia lay quiet in the onion-scented room. By the next day she was well enough to walk in the garden and the 10 days of being trapped in the house made her impatient.

"The good doctor's medicines have cured you of the plague," Nurse said on the morning of the tenth day.

"Perhaps I didn't have the plague," Lucia said. "Perhaps I had a chill."

"I felt the deadly swelling for myself, Mistress Lucia," Nurse said briskly.

The girl's eyes pricked with tears as she remembered Mousie. She hoped the doctor found him and gave him a good burial.

"Can we go to the market today?" she asked.

"We can," Nurse said. "It will be good to get out into the streets and the crowds again."

But when they stepped through the gate of their house and walked down into the town they saw no crowds.

Some houses had their shutters fastened tight and red crosses were daubed across the doors. Other doors lay open and the darkened houses were empty. Thin dogs scavenged for scraps in the filth of the gutters and scrawny cows in paddocks cried to be milked.

Lucia and the nanny stared at the desolate main street. Then a cracked bell clacked and a voice cried, "Bring out your dead!"

A cart appeared in the marketplace. The driver was hunched over the reins and his partner walked behind. The cart was piled with a stinking cargo of corpses. Lucia and the nanny watched as the carter stopped and waved a filthy hand towards an empty doorway. The corpse-collector walked across to where a man lay dead. The man was dressed in a black cloak and he held a bunch of violets in his white hand.

"Another dead 'un," the collector called.

"Anything in his pockets?" the driver asked.

The man pushed a hand in and said, "Gold! It's full of gold!"

"Let's have it," the driver cried. "It won't do him much good where he's going!"

The corpse-collector gave a long moan of disgust. "And look at this!" he said pulling a bundle of fur from the pocket.

"Mousie!" the watching Lucia whispered.

"What is it?" the driver called to his partner.

"A rat! A dead black rat! What would he want with a thing like that?"

"Don't know. But we'll bury him and his pet rat together."

The doctor's body was dragged on to the cart, which was turned towards the graveyard.

"His medicines didn't save him," Lucia said to Nurse Del Arte as they retreated to the safety of their home.

"When Mister Death comes for you there's nothing on earth will save you," Nurse said. "Nothing."

The Black Death

Of all the disasters in the history of the world the Black Death is perhaps the most horrific. It killed 25 million people across the known world in just over 300 years – that was one person out of every three in Europe at the time.

No one understood the disease. It was spread by fleas. The fleas sucked the blood of black rats and the rats died of the plague. The fleas then needed a new source of fresh blood. If there was a human being close by the flea would jump on to them and infect them too.

It seems to have started in central Asia in 1334 but really began to spread when an invading army besieged the town of Kaffa (now Feodoiya in Southern Russia). The soldiers of the invading army began dying so their generals had the rotten corpses catapulted over the walls into the enemy town. Italians in the city escaped from Kaffa but took the plague back to Europe with them.

The plague crossed the Channel to England in 1349. Scottish Border raiders were delighted to see their English enemies suffering and they attacked. Their "reward" was to carry the plague back to Scotland with them.

Plague "cures"

No one could cure the disease, but many tried to make money by claiming they had cures. These included:

1. Human sewage was collected and worn around the neck in a bag. The smell was foul but doctors believed the smell would be strong enough to drive out the rotten plague air.

2. Patients were advised to bathe in urine. Again, the stink was supposed to drive out the infection. Really it could give the patient other diseases.

3. Leeches were placed on the body to suck out "bad" blood. This would weaken the plague victim and simply speed their death. Dried toads or dried lizards were placed on plague sores to draw out the poison. But once the plague sores were erupting it was too late to help.

4. Butter and lard were rubbed into the purple swellings. The blood of puppies or pigeons was rubbed into the forehead.

5. Boils were sliced open and red-hot pokers were pushed into the open wounds. If the plague didn't kill the patient then the shock of this treatment often did!

6. Patients were given the poison arsenic to eat. Again, the cure could kill if the disease didn't.

7. Rooms of plague victims were "purified" by placing a plate of fresh milk or a bowl of onions in the middle of the room.

8. Swallowing crushed emeralds was an expensive way to die. Of course, the fake doctors didn't really use emeralds – but it was an excuse to charge as much money as they could.

Some disasters strike violently and suddenly so the victims die before they really understand what is happening. But the Black Death was more terrifying. It was invisible and silent. You could see people suffering all around and do nothing but wait for your turn … or, if you were one of the lucky ones, wait until it passed.

What sort of life is that? Waiting, terrified, for old Mister Death to knock on your door and touch you with his scythe.

EPILOGUE

People have been interested in disasters since the dawn of time. One of the oldest stories to survive is about the time when the whole Earth was flooded.

And people are still interested in disasters. Newspapers report them, books and films are made about them. Disasters test people to their breaking point and every disaster seems to bring fresh examples of heroes and villians. Take this simple story...

A ship sails across the Atlantic and hits an obstruction. It begins to sink. There are not enough lifeboats for everyone so the captain orders, "Women and children first!"

What would have happened to you if you'd been a child on that ship?

If you had been on the ship *Arctic* in 1854 then you would have died. The crew ran to the armoury and grabbed weapons. They held the women and children at gunpoint – women who tried to save themselves were thrown into the icy sea. Not one woman or child survived.

If you had been on the ship *Titanic* almost 60 years later, you may well have survived – 50 per cent of the 105 children lived because so many men courageously gave up their places in the lifeboats. Take the eight men in the ship's band, for example. They played dance music to calm the passengers as those passengers climbed into the boats. As the water flowed around their feet, the band played a final hymn. Then there was silence. None of the eight musicians was saved.

How would you behave? Like a crewman on the *Arctic*? Or like a bandsman on the *Titanic*?

Hopefully you'll never find out.

But that's why we are so fascinated by disasters. They show the best of human behaviour, they show the worst.

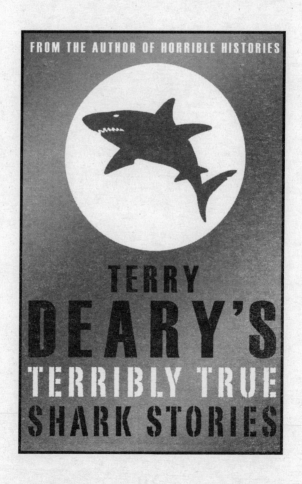